UNSOLVED MYSTERIES
OF SEA AND SHORE

Also by Edward Rowe Snow

True Tales of Terrible Shipwrecks

Women of the Sea

Mysterious Tales of the New England Coast

New England Sea Tragedies

Piracy, Mutiny and Murder

Great Sea Rescues and Tales of Survival

Legends of the New England Coast

The Vengeful Sea

Famous Lighthouses of America

Amazing Sea Stories Never Told Before

True Tales of Pirates and Their Gold

Great Gales and Dire Disasters

True Tales of Buried Treasure

Unsolved

Mysteries

of Sea

and Shore

by Edward Rowe Snow

ILLUSTRATED

DODD, MEAD & COMPANY, NEW YORK

Library of Congress Catalog Card Number: 63-22489

Printed in the United States of America
by The Cornwall Press, Inc., Cornwall, N. Y.

TO WALT EHRENFELD

OF YORK,

PENNSYLVANIA,

WHOSE INTEREST IN

STORIES OF THE SEA

IS DEEP AND SINCERE

Introduction

When my book *True Tales of Terrible Shipwrecks* was published early this Fall, I was ready with this volume, which has been forming in my mind for more than ten years. My forty-first book, *Unsolved Mysteries of Sea and Shore,* reflects the thoughts of the poet Lord Byron, who wrote so understandingly of the sea in his *Childe Harold's Pilgrimage.* He speaks for all of us who love but fear the ocean and expresses our wonder and respect for the trackless wastes of the deep:

> Roll on, thou deep and dark blue ocean—roll!
> Ten thousand fleets sweep over thee in vain;
> Man marks the earth with ruin; his control
> Stops with the shore; upon the watery plain
> The wrecks are all thy deed, nor doth remain
> A shadow of man's ravage, save his own,
> When for a moment, like a drop of rain,
> He sinks into thy depths with bubbling groan,
> Without a grave, unknelled, uncoffined and unknown.
>
> . . . .
>
> The image of Eternity—the throne
> Of the Invisible; even from out thy slime
> The monsters of the deep are made; each zone
> Obeys thee; thou goest forth, dread, fathomless, **alone.**

Man has long been fascinated—and perplexed—by enigmas of the sea. This volume contains those mysteries which simply cannot be solved, no matter how we try.

Those whose help in the preparation of this book was outstanding include Mary E. Brown, Avis G. Clarke, Walter E. Ehrenfeld, Margaret Hackett, Mary Hamer, Marie Hansen, Laurence P. Macdonald, William McIntire, Muriel McKenzie, Lawrence Rideout, Andrea Smyth, Dorothy Caroline Snow, Winthrop James Snow, Mrs. James E. Sumner, Barbara Whitledge, and Howard White.

I am deeply grateful to others who wish to remain unmentioned in this list of acknowledgments.

Substantial assistance was furnished by the following institutions: The Bostonian Society, the Boston Athenaeum, the Boston Public Library, the Massachusetts Historical Society, the U. S. Navy, the U. S. Coast Guard, the National Archives, the Harvard College Library, the Peabody Museum, the Essex Institute, and the American Antiquarian Society.

My particular thanks go to Commander George G. Bailey, USN, Captain of the U.S.S. *Preserver,* who made it possible for me to go aboard the *Trieste,* and to his brother, John S. Bailey, of Northeastern University.

Anna-Myrle, my wife, read each chapter with care and attention, and often worked many more hours than she should have to finish this volume with me on time. I publicly acknowledge my deep appreciation for her efforts.

EDWARD ROWE SNOW

Contents

Illustrations

CHAPTER 1

Mysteries of the Everglades

More than ten years ago I made arrangements with a treasure seeker from Belmont, Massachusetts, to let him take my Fisher metal detector down to the Everglades with him in a search for buried gold. It was a long time before I saw my detector again, but what disappointed me more than anything else was the treasure seeker's reluctance to tell me of his adventures. In my book *Buried Treasure* there is a picture of a substantial pile of the gold and silver coins which this gentleman has collected. As regards this particular trip to Florida, however, he has always been strangely silent.

Nevertheless, I have been able to get together quite a little information about Everglades treasures. Many of the stories I have ferreted out have mysteries which probably will never be solved, and other unusual tales have vital parts of the accounts so obscured that they have eluded my most careful and painstaking research.

Physically the state of Florida thrusts downward from the

American continent toward the great island of Cuba like a finger which is eternally pointing south. Most of Florida is flat and sandy with occasional forests of pines. There are a few lakes, large and small, but the southern end is almost one vast swamp, the area known as the Everglades.

In all the world there is no stranger place than this gigantic morass, for the location is an enormous saw-grass mire fringed by cypress swamps, the passageways through which are dangerous and hard to remember.

The Everglades is really a wide lake dotted with islands on which live many white people and substantial numbers of Seminole Indians. Banks of tall grass rise from the shallow water, the harsh gray-green blades forming an impenetrable jungle. Fish, alligators, snakes, and that strange water-beast, the manatee,* are inhabitants of the region.

The unsolved enigma of the Spanish galleon is but one of many strange mysteries which have their location in the Everglades. More than three centuries ago, if we are to believe the local traditions, a Spanish galleon was caught in a hurricane off the Florida coast and swept inland on the crest of a tremendous tidal wave. Driven far into the swamp, she capsized. There she lay for two and a quarter centuries. Creepers covered her, and trees forced their way through her rotting timbers. In 1859 two fishermen named Cato Jenkins and Mark Smith came across a curious vine-covered mound, and decided to explore it.

Cato, striking at the mound with a boat hook, found it was substantially solid underneath. Breaking through timbers, they found a dark wooden corridor which apparently led to the inner areas of the huge vessel. Exploring in the darkness,

* Believed to be the origin of the mermaid legend.

Cato was thrilled when he discovered several golden doubloons. Just as he was showing them to Mark he stepped on
a cottonmouth moccasin, and the snake sank its fangs into
Cato's bare leg. Mark carried him into the boat and rowed
away for help, but Cato died a short time later.

When Mark told his story of the galleon he showed the
doubloons to prove his tale, but most of his listeners, with
the fate of Cato in their minds, were afraid to go with him.
Later Mark and a fisherman named Angelo Mizell went after
the treasure, but they never found it. Mark had taken no
bearings, and there are few landmarks in the Everglades.
This mystery of the lost galleon is still an unsolved enigma
of Florida.

Another Everglades treasure story concerns the notorious
pirate Jack Rackam, about whom I wrote in 1944.* Before
he finished his career Rackam had become one of those creatures in whom such qualities as kindness and compassion
are completely lacking. In reality he was a fiend in human
form. In the year 1718, two weeks after Blackbeard had been
slain in his fight with Captain Maynard, Rackam was marooned on the West Indian island of Haiti. Deciding to turn
pirate, he scoured the taverns of Port au Prince and soon
collected thirty men who agreed to go "on the account" with
him.

About this time Rackam met a woman pirate, Mary Read,
with whom he fell in love in his own rough way. They became partners in piracy. One day he decided to question her
about pirates in general, for he could not understand how
she could be interested in the profession.

"Why do you follow a line of life that exposes you to so

* *Pirates and Buccaneers*, pp. 300–306.

much danger, and at last to the almost certainty of being hanged?" asked Rackam. Her reply was typical of her unusual life, and greatly surprised him.

"As to hanging, I think it no great hardship, for were it not for that, every cowardly fellow would turn pirate, and so infest the seas that men of courage would starve. If it were my choice, I would not have the punishment less than death, the fear of which kept some dastardly rogues honest. Many of those who are now cheating widows and orphans and oppressing their poor neighbors who have no money to obtain justice would then rob at sea, and the ocean would be as crowded with rogues as the land, so that no merchant would venture out, and the trade in a little time would not be worth following."

Ann Bonney, another woman pirate, joined Rackam and Mary Read. The three were successful in their piratical expeditions even beyond their fondest hopes, and soon there was so much booty about that they realized it would be necessary to go ashore and find a good hiding place for it. Discovering a perfect location near a small out-of-the-way bay on the Cuban coast, they sailed in. Far from any settlement, the mouth of the bay was narrow, with deep water inside. Here they built huts, surrounded them with an earth fort, and mounted three cannon. From this stronghold Rackam sailed out to loot passing ships. Still he was not satisfied with his settlement as a location where he could bury treasure.

While at sea Rackam vowed that he would find a hiding place into which no warship would be likely to blunder. Sailing northward, he reached the Gulf coast of Florida, along which he proceeded until he reached Oyster Bay. A small but deep river coming out of the Glades enters the head of this bay. Manning his sweeps he passed up the river, a distance of some ten miles, and entered the great swamp. As it was the rainy season, he found that there was plenty of water. Discovering an island which suited his fancy, Rackam buried his stolen gold; then he and his crew of ruffians dropped back toward the sea and made for the trade routes.

In 1720 news came to him of a large Spanish ship, the *St. Joseph,* which was carrying a great cargo of gold in bars from Colon to Spain, and he decided to capture her. Early one morning in August the lookout in the crow's-nest sighted her, and his helmsman began the chase.

Toward night the wind fell, and both ships floated idly on an ocean of glass. Rackam had his sweeps manned, but the unfortunate Spaniard had no sweeps. Just before daylight the pirate ship stole up out of the shadows upon the tall Spaniard, and Rackam's men leaped aboard like wolves. The Spaniards fought bravely but were no match for Rackam's savage crew. Within half an hour the last of them fell, and the battle ended. The galleon had about $2,170,000 in gold aboard. Rackam's men wished to divide and scatter, but their captain swore that he would double this sum before quitting the sea.

Rackam put a prize crew aboard the *St. Joseph* and both craft headed for Oyster Bay. Unloading his gold, he took it in boats to his secret hiding place in the Everglades, where all of it was carefully buried. Then once more he returned to the open sea, sailing forth in command of the heavily armed *St. Joseph.*

Rackem now became an international menace, and the governor of Jamaica vowed that it was full time to put an end to this ruffian's piracies. One day early in 1720, Captain Jack found himself caught by a Spanish man-of-war on Cuba, where he had been careening his vessel. The dons warped their great battleship into the channel that evening, completely blocking all possibility of the ship's escape. Rackam told the two women that the game was up, and they prepared to sell their lives dearly. Nearby the Spanish man-of-war, just a little further out to sea, was a small English sloop which had been captured as an interloper in Spanish waters. A prize crew was then aboard.

Rackam called his fellow pirates together to explain his plan. They would launch their longboat, into which everything of value would be placed, and row in the dead of the night far to the south of the man-of-war, after which they would come up on the English sloop and capture the prize crew. The program was carried out without a mishap. Captain Jack and his crew soon were aboard their prize, where they quickly silenced the Spanish crew, slipped cable, and sailed triumphantly out to sea. The following morning the Spanish man-of-war opened fire upon the pirate's ship, but in a short time they discovered the true state of affairs and cursed themselves for the fools they had been.

Rackam had escaped this time, but his hourglass was slowly running out. In August, 1720, he went to sea again, capturing several small craft and eventually reaching Harbor Island, where the pirates stole fishing nets and tackle from schooners anchored offshore. Sailing across to Hispaniola, they killed and ate many cattle from several French settlements along the coast. On the nineteenth of October off the island of Jamaica they captured a schooner which was commanded by Master Thomas Spenlow. Reaching Dry Harbor

Bay the next day, Captain Rackam stood in and fired a gun, causing the men on a sloop at the wharf to run ashore, but when they found out it was Captain Jack they all came back, and even asked to be signed on.

Sailing around the western point of the island at Point Negril, Rackam came upon a small native craft and invited the men to come aboard for a drink of punch. All nine members of the crew of the dugout accepted the invitation, coming on board fully armed, however. After a few drinks they put down their muskets and pulled off their cutlasses, deciding to enjoy their drinking without encumbrances.

At that very minute a sloop which had been outfitted by the governor of Jamaica sighted the pirate ship and started at once in pursuit. The pirate lookout noticed the sloop, standing directly for them, and reported the state of affairs to Rackam. Handsome Jack ordered the anchor weighed at once. Captain Barnet, commander of the armed sloop, rapidly overhauled the pirate ship, whose captain soon realized this was one vessel from which he could not escape.

The sloop caught the pirate ship and boarded it. A bloody engagement followed, but the soldiers and marines were too strong for the buccaneers. After a few quick skirmishes most of the pirate crew ran below decks. There were three exceptions, Ann Bonney, Mary Read, and another pirate whose name is not known. Captain Jack, to the scorn of Ann Bonney, fled below with the others. Without question Mary Read and Ann Bonney were braver than any other pirates aboard the ship that day, fighting on long after the other buccaneers had gone. The two women only surrendered after the hopelessness of their situation was realized. All the buccaneers were brought to Port Royal, Jamaica, given a quick trial, and sentenced to be hanged.

On November 15, 1720, Captain Rackam was allowed to visit Ann Bonney. Expecting her to commiserate with him, Rackam was amazed when she began to scold her lover.

"I am sorry to see you there, Jack," said Ann, "but if you had fought like a man, you need not have been hanged like a dog." These were her last words to the man she loved, for the following day, November 16, Captain Jack Rackam was hanged at Gallows Point, Port Royal, along with eight of his crew. The nine men who had gone aboard Rackam's vessel for a drink were also finally sentenced to be executed.

Ann Bonney and Mary Read, then in prison, announced that they were expectant mothers. Therefore their execution was put off until such time as they could be properly hanged. Poor Mary, however, grew sick in jail and died, her thoughts to the last of the handsome young navigator who ended his career at Gallows Point, Jamaica. Ann, more fortunate, outlived her companion and actually disappeared from the prison about a year later. All we are sure of is that she was not executed, but whether her child was born in prison or out, the records of Jamaica do not tell.

At the time of Rackam's execution, he and the other pirates were offered freedom should they reveal the location of their treasure in the Everglades. Each pirate in turn was questioned and told that his life would be spared if he would reveal the secret of the hiding place. Each in turn vowed that he would be damned if he betrayed his trust. So they were hanged without speaking, and to this day the site of Rackam's cache remains a secret.

CHAPTER 2

Jenkins and His Ear

While in England in the year 1944 I first began a detailed study of the so-called War of Jenkins' Ear. As I was totally deaf for a brief period after returning to England from the North African Theatre of War, the controversial question of how Jenkins lost his ear particularly appealed to me.

Of course, I had studied the story of Jenkins and his ear in high school and later at Harvard, but I would never have done research on the subject but for that period of convalescence at Frenchay Hospital in Bristol.

Captain Jenkins might be compared to the gentleman whose sole claim to fame lay in the fact that he sat in the House of Commons for years and spoke but once. Jenkins will always be remembered only for the loss of his ear, but it caused a war. There are those, however, who question the entire story, claiming that Jenkins never lost his ear at all.

The British writer L. G. Lockhard, who died in 1960, initially gave me the suggestion that Jenkins was a man of mystery. First Jenkins was a sailor, then he became the captain of his ship, still dater he is reputed to have had his ear removed, and then he is swallowed up by the passing of years.

He made so little impression on the writers of his generation that it is hard to find any evidence of just what sort of man he really was. For one period in his life he was the most interesting character in all London. Then the days went by, his moment of importance became a memory, and still later the memory itself was forgotten.

Let us now examine the historical background to the international situation in 1738. Opposed by men of courage and boldness, British Prime Minister Robert Walpole lost most of his friends in his fight to keep control of the government. An unscrupulous leader, Walpole was almost universally hated. Several brilliant men in England took sides against him—the elder Pitt, Carteret, and Bolingbroke, to name three. He overcame them not by his oratory, for he was not a good speaker, and not by his learning, for it did not exist. Walpole won out over others because of his careful, scientific use of corruption and graft.

Until 1738, Walpole's strength lay in the division of his enemies. The Tories, the Jacobites, the Hanoverians, the Whig Opposition, and the young Whig "Patriots"—all these different factions were united in their hatred of Walpole, but they had little else in common until the year 1738 when Captain Jenkins stepped into the picture.

Since the Treaty of Utrecht English relations with Spain had been steadily deteriorating. Under the terms of the peace, a commercial treaty was incorporated which gave the South Sea Company a thirty-year contract to supply the Spanish colonies with Negro slaves. Also the treaty made arrangements for the annual dispatching to these colonies of one ship with European merchandise. Unfortunately the new arrangement simply did not work. English merchants soon discovered that the trading of the old days, illegal though it was, had been a much safer and more profitable business than was the new enforced system. Accordingly they decided to resort to all kinds of subterfuge. As their ships were allowed refitting and provisioning in Spanish ports, it was not difficult on such occasions to drop a cargo. There was also plenty of smuggling going on.

In the old days all this would not have mattered much. But the new Spanish government sent out instructions that their coast guard sailors should board and search any vessels suspected of smuggling goods into the Spanish colonies. The sailors were none too careful of their methods and were often unnecessarily rough with the crew of the ships they boarded. Not only did they punish the captains of vessels caught actually smuggling, but they were harsh with the masters of ships merely suspected of smuggling. Indeed, many English craft and crews suffered savage treatment at the hands of the Spaniards.

Fifty-two British merchant ships were taken or plundered by the Spaniards in a ten-year period beginning in 1728. A Rhode Island sloop named *Runlet,* whose master was Captain Brin, was boarded by the Spanish sailors and her men treated barbarously. The Spaniards burned the fingers of their captives with lighted matches to get confessions, and most of the time there was nothing to confess.

The stories, of course, lost nothing in the telling, and after a time people began to believe that no English vessel was safe in South American waters and that the Spanish prisons were packed with unfortunate British and American seamen, torn from their lawful pursuits at the bidding of that tyrant, the king of Spain. However, in spite of the efforts of the coast guard, the smuggling continued; and probably neither side had a monopoly on atrocities.*

In 1737 it is possible that Walpole might have worked out a satisfactory solution to the problem of keeping the two nations at peace if the Opposition in Parliament had not decided to capitalize on the situation and agitate against Spain. Who were the Spaniards, they shouted, to capture British ships and British seamen, torturing them in the bargain?

And so it was that on October 11, 1737, a large group complained to King George II about the increasing Spanish attacks. The usual steps were taken, and Madrid was notified. On March 3, 1738, the Opposition attacked the government again with speeches and more resolutions. Backed into a corner, Walpole gave in and promised to investigate. Lord Mansfield of the Opposition now drew colorful pictures of poor British seamen "rotting in jail," and several of the so-called victims appeared at the bar of the House. It is believed that they fundamentally told the truth concerning the atrocities to which they had been subjected, but they probably exaggerated their tales.

Of course, Captain Jenkins' ear was the best of all the testimonials. When summoned to speak in the House, Jenkins explained how seven years before he had sailed from Jamaica to England in a Scottish sloop, the *Rebecca,* on a

---

* During this period the Spaniards claimed that two gentlemen of Spain were shut up aboard an English craft and that the nose and ears of one Spaniard were cut off!

perfectly legitimate voyage. Off Havana she was boarded by a Spanish coast-guard frigate, whose captain, Fandino by name, found all in order. Nevertheless, Jenkins was most savagely abused, and the captain tore off Jenkins' ear, telling the latter to take the ear to his king with the message, "If your King George were present, I'd cut his ears off, too." Then and there Jenkins decided to follow the suggestion of Captain Fandino to the letter. Obtaining a bottle, he filled it with preservative and put his ear in the container. Reaching England, he bought a new suit and then presented himself at the king's palace. He carefully told King George his unusual story, after which he removed his severed ear from the bottle and showed it to his Sovereign.

The king listened carefully and looked with interest at the ear, but he took no action against the Spanish. The weeks went by, then the months, and finally the years. Still the king did nothing as seven long years passed. Jenkins was then asked to show his ear to the House of Commons. It made a great sensation, and when the people heard of it, Spain was denounced.

Jenkins' ear became a war cry against Spain. Even the great poet Alexander Pope became interested. Writing a poem about the Spaniards, Pope mentioned that they "cropped our ears and sent them to the king!" The Commons now assured the king of the support of the House in whatever he might decide to do against Spain.

Walpole did not wish a war, but almost all the remainder of the country did. It seemed for a time that he would weather the storm. A convention was prepared and actually signed by both countries, arranging reparations and an inquiry into grievances; but England as a whole simply did not wish peace, and the people were in a dangerous mood. All during this crisis Jenkins was showing his severed ear around London.

When an attempt at conciliation was made, the Spanish court, offended by insults and mindful of the arrival of Admiral Haddock's squadron in the Mediterranean, became difficult. On October 19, 1739, with neither England nor Spain yielding, Walpole made a simple statement. "They may ring their bells now"—as the sounds of rejoicing fell on his ears—"before long they will be wringing their hands." War was declared.

And what of Jenkins, the man who did so much to make the war inevitable? Now the conflict had begun, he all but vanished from history.*

Did Jenkins tell the truth about his ear? Many people believed that the whole affair had been arranged to damage Walpole and that Jenkins had actually lost his ear in the pillory. Burke called the affair the "fable of Jenkins' ear." Horace Walpole also commented in 1761 that the truth was that Jenkins "died wtih both ears on his head." One account stated that no trace of his appearing at the bar of the House has ever been discovered in the journals. On the other hand, the House journal entry for March 16, 1738, orders Captain Robert Jenkins to "attend the House immediately." Of course, it could be said that he never appeared. Hardly had Walpole fallen from power when the general opinion seemed to be that Jenkins had been an impostor.

For the fact finders, from the list of the fifty-two British craft mentioned earlier in this chapter, we read: "The *Re-*

* In 1740 we find him supervisor of the East India Company's affairs at St. Helena, where he became governor for a short time.

becca, Robert Jenkins, Jamaica to London, boarded and plundered near the Havana." I admit that the list was published in 1738 when the ear controversy had started and the entry may have been a political move, but at least it is, without question, on record.

In the *Gentleman's Magazine* for June, 1731, is printed the following:

The *Rebecca,* Captain Jenkins, was taken in her passage from Jamaica by a Spanish Guarda Costa, who put her people to the torture; part of which was that they hanged up the Captain three times, one with the cabin-boy at his feet; they then cut off one of his ears, took away his candles and instruments, and detained him a whole day. Being then dismissed, the Captain bore away for the Havana,* which, the Spaniards perceiving, stood after her, and declared that if she did not immediately go for the Gulf, they would set the ship on fire; to which they were forced to submit, and after many hardships and perils, arrived in the river Thames, June 11th. The Captain has since been at Court, and laid his case before his Majesty.

The above would indicate that Jenkins did not create the story in 1738 for the Opposition. The account in the *Gentleman's Magazine,* moreover, is confirmed by some official correspondence unearthed by Professor J. K. Laughton and published in the *English Historical Review* of October, 1889. That year, Professor Laughton did substantial research on Captain Jenkins and uncovered documentary evidence. In a letter he discovered which was dated September 12, 1731, Rear Admiral Charles Stewart formally complained to the

* Known today as Havana, Cuba.

governor of Havana of the treatment accorded to Jenkins. Stewart stated that he

. . . was in the hopes that you would have made use of your power to have detected and discouraged the violence and villainies which has for a long time been practised by those you distinguish by the name of Guarda Costas; but as you don't take the least notice to answer that part of my letter, and that I have repeated assurances that you allow vessels to be fitted out of your harbour particularly Fandino, and others who have committed the most cruel piratical outrages on several ships and vessels of the King my master's subjects, particularly about the 20th of April last sailed out of your harbour in one of these Guarda Costas, and met a ship of this island bound for England; and after using the Captain in a most barbarous inhuman manner, taking all his money, cutting off one of his ears, plundering him of those necessaries which were to carry the ship home.

Professor Laughton's final discovery was a dispatch of June, 1742. Captain Thomas Frankland, of H.M.S. *Rose,* sent a letter to the Admiralty, reporting an engagement with four Spanish ships, one of which was a snow.*

"The Captain of the snow is Juan de Leon Fandino," wrote Frankland, "and has had a commission from the King since 1719, in all which time he was never before taken. He is the man who commanded the Guard of Coast out of Havana that took Jenkins when his ear was cut off."

I have now presented all the evidence in this strange mystery of the ear of one Captain Robert Jenkins.

---

* A vessel which is rigged as a brig, but has a third mast close abaft the main.

Mr. Lockhard, with whom I conversed in 1943, was fascinated by the possibility that Jenkins may have roamed the streets of London from 1731 to 1738 exhibiting his ear at the slightest request. How did Jenkins employ the seven years between 1731 and 1738? Did he pass from coffeehouse to coffeehouse and from great man to great man, with his ear and his story, until at last his patience was rewarded? Who was the genius who discovered his potential value to His Majesty's Opposition? Who stage-managed his appearance in the House of Commons? How accurate were the particulars of the tale he told there? And how far was he primed by interested parties?

One can only surmise what the answers to these questions can be. The main enigma, whether or not his ear was cut off, can never be satisfactorily solved. For my part, I think that Jenkins did lose his ear. How it happened, of course, is another matter.

CHAPTER 3

La Pérouse's *Boussole* and *Astrolabe*

In 1783, with the coming of peace again between England and France, the latter country, although almost bankrupt, decided to challenge England's supremacy on the high seas. In 1785 two great frigates, the *Boussole* and the *Astrolabe,* were sent on an expedition to the South Seas under the command of a great French naval officer, Comte Jean François de Galaup de La Pérouse. At the time, he was forty-four years of age, with his chief claim to fame a successful raid in 1782 on the British outpost of Hudson Bay.

In dispatches written by M. Milet-Mureau, we find that the flagship of the two-craft fleet was the *Boussole* with La Pérouse himself aboard while Vicomte de Langle was the master of the *Astrolabe.* The entire ship's company in both vessels numbered 223.

The king of France, Louis XVI, gave La Pérouse orders for the expedition. We read that it was a scientific journey across the Pacific Ocean in which the islands were to be charted, natives studied, flora and fauna listed, and commercial possibilities noted. In a book written about the expedition it is stated that La Pérouse

. . . will study with zeal and interest every means of improving their condition, by supplying them with the vegetables, fruits and useful trees of Europe; by showing them how to sow and cultivate them; and by teaching them to make the best use of these gifts, the object of which is to multiply those products which are essential to people who draw almost their entire livelihood from the soil.

The plans of Louis XVI were worthy and ambitious. "His Majesty would consider it one of the happiest triumphs of the enterprise, were it to be concluded without costing the life of a single man," was the comment of the French king. With these admonitions from the king himself, what happened on the voyage was indeed ironic.

The ships crossed the equator on September 29, 1785, and early in 1786 rounded Cape Horn. For the next two years the *Boussole* and the *Astrolabe* cruised up and down the Pacific and were successful in their explorations.

In the early summer of 1786 La Pérouse started for Alaska, and on June 23 the expedition sighted Mount Saint Elias there. A harbor which closely resembled Toulon in France was discovered, and the two ships almost were wrecked at the entrance. The usual soundings were taken as they approached the harbor, but when the officer in charge continued the soundings into an area of high surf and the boat capsized, twenty-one men drowned. La Pérouse, deeply shocked and depressed by the tragedy, sailed away from the place they had named Port des Français and sailed to California.

On September 7 he had crossed the Pacific again and landed a representative at Kamchatka with French dispatches. Arriving in Samoa on December 6, Captain de Langle took four boats ashore to get fresh water. While they were filling their casks with water, de Langle gave several of the natives presents, but soon there were more than four hundred savages crowding around the boats, and great excitement developed.

The islanders held the lines attached to the anchors, and the captain ordered his men to fire over their heads. "A shower of stones poured down on us and the battle became general. Those whose muskets were in a condition to go off brought down several of the enemy, but did not succeed in deterring the others. One party made for the boats, while another, numbering five or six hundred, kept up a terrible fusillade of stones." Vicomte de Langle was killed, and only two barges escaped, while most of the men aboard were badly wounded by the rocks and stones. Possibly La Pérouse should have retaliated, but he recalled the admonitions of the king not to punish any islanders and sailed away.

On January 26, 1788, he arrived at Botany Bay, where he found the British squadron under the command of Governor Phillip. Remaining in the bay for almost a month, when he left he handed the British commander dispatches which he asked be delivered to the king of France. These dispatches were the last word ever heard from La Pérouse. A final sentence from them follows:

Toward the end of July 1788, I shall pass between New Guinea and New Holland, by a different channel than Endeavour Strait, provided such a one exist. During the month of September and a part of October I shall visit the Gulf of Carpentaria, and all the west coast of New Holland, as far as Van Diemen's Land; but yet in such a manner that it may be possible for me to get to the northward in time to arrive at the Isle of France in the beginning of December 1788.

Finally, after the anchors of the two craft were weighed, the *Boussole* and the *Astrolabe* sailed out of Botany Bay. Thus they disappeared forever with not a man aboard either craft ever seen again.

When La Pérouse's message reached France, the French Revolution was in full swing. After a reasonable amount of time, however, with no further word from the navigator, another two craft were sent out in search of the missing expedition. Named the *Recherche* and the *Esperance,* the vessels left Brest on December 28, 1791. Evidently the leader of the expedition, General d'Entrecasteaux, was misled after reaching the Cape of Good Hope by claims that natives on the Admiralty Islands were dressed in French uniforms, possibly from the ships of La Pérouse.* D'Entrecasteaux decided to sail to the Admiralty Islands, but when he arrived there he found not a trace of either French uniforms or news of the lost expedition. For two years d'Entrecasteaux sailed around the southern Pacific. Finally, his provisions were exhausted, and the crew came down with scurvy. D'En-

* See M. Labillardiere, *An Account of a Voyage in Search of La Pérouse,* London, 1800.

trecasteaux died of the illness a few months later. On May 20, 1792, the expedition passed the island of Vanikoro.* Survivors of the two lost craft actually were alive on the island then; but the searchers saw no evidence of anyone ashore there, and reasoned it would be wasting time to land.

When they reached Surabaya in the Dutch Colony of Java, they were made prisoners, as war had broken out between France and Holland. Some time later survivors of the d'Entrecasteaux expedition were sent to the Isle of France, and efforts to find La Pérouse were abandoned for the time.

Most of the mystery as to what happened to La Pérouse will never be solved. Nevertheless the curtain was drawn apart just a little some time later. In 1812 a ship, the *Hunter,* was sailing from New South Wales. Aboard were Captain Robson, in command, and a mate named Pierre Dillon. The chief officer was a Mr. Norman.

When the *Hunter* reached Vilear Bay, in the Fiji Islands, on February 19, 1813, Robson was welcomed by the island chief, as the captain had collected sandalwood at Vilear Bay on several previous occasions. The chief, however, had bad news. Robson would not be able to gather sandalwood in the usual way, as a bloody tribal war had broken out on the island.

The two men came to an agreement. Captain Robson would help win the war for the chief if the natives would load the *Hunter* with sandalwood afterward. Everyone went ashore. Mate Dillon, who wrote about it later, discovered that there were several Americans and Englishmen living on the island. They were there to attempt the recovery of Amer-

* Also called Mannicolo and Malicolo.

ican dollars which went down in the wreck of an American brig lost off the island in 1808.*

The deciding battle of the war saw Robson actively participating in an attack on Nanpacab, six miles up the river from Vilear. Accompanied by forty-six canoes, his three armed boats, each carrying twenty musketeers and a mounted two-pound cannon, swung the battle to the chief's side, and a considerable number of the local Nanpacab warriors were killed.†

With the allies having won a clear-cut victory, the loading of sandalwood aboard the *Hunter* began. Unhappily the chief began to shirk his agreement. May, June, July, and August went by with only 150 tons of sandalwood put aboard, and Captain Robson realized he would eventually have a fight on his hands to get the *Hunter* loaded. Changing his attitude toward the natives who had formerly been his faithful allies, Robson realized that he would have to show his strength. On the morning of September 6, arming all the Europeans with muskets, he placed them under the direction of Mr. Norman, the first officer. Going ashore at a location called the Black Rock, Norman's group began plans to build a fort ashore.

Mate Pierre Dillon feared an ambush and warned his chief, but Norman ignored him, A short time later the chief officer and his men were walking along a narrow path when several natives appeared and attempted to stop the Europeans. One

---

* The rumor that there were several hundred of the rare 1804-dated United States dollars aboard the brig cannot be substantiated in any way. Forty thousand dollars in all, however, went down with the 1808 brig shipwreck and have never been recovered. The actual dates on the coins are unknown.

† Their bodies were dissected, baked, and eaten by the chief's warriors soon afterward.

was shot dead, and Norman ordered the chief's house to be sett afire. Meanwhile shrieks were heard, and Dillon realized what had happened. The natives were ambushing and killing white men all over the island. The chief officer now told his group that they would have to fight their way back to the boats. Retreating through the woods, they found dead Europeans all around them.

Reaching the top of a precipice where a path led down to the beach and their boat, they noticed a large band of savages at the bottom of the cliff. Already having smeared their bodies with the blood of their victims from the *Hunter,* the cannibals confidently awaited the white men's approach. Suddenly, halfway down the precipice Norman gave a terrible cry of anguish, for a lance had pierced his body. A native had followed the Europeans down the path and killed their leader. Dillon fired his musket at the native and had the satisfaction of seeing him fall.

Reloading, Dillon turned around to find that all his other men had scattered. Descending to the foot of the precipice, he saw another group of his companions. There was a great hill ahead, with a mighty rock on top some distance away.

"Take the hill! Take the hill!" he cried out and ran up it. Clambering on top of the rock, he was joined by Charles Savage, a Chinese named Luis, Martin Bushart, Thomas Daphne, and William Wilson.*

Fortunately, the rock to which they escaped was so steep that only a few could climb it at the same time, and it was so high that it was difficult for the natives to annoy them much with spears or slings. When the natives shot several

* The first three mentioned above resided on the island and the latter two were seamen from the *Hunter.*

arrows at the men, a strong gale of wind blew the missiles off their intended course. Dillon's story follows:

Our chief officer having fallen, I now, as next in rank, took command of the party, and stationed them in the best way I could to defend our post. I did not allow more than one or two muskets to be fired at a time, and kept the wounded man loading for us. Several of the natives ascended the hill to within a few yards, and were shot by us in self-defence as fast as they approached. After some of them had been killed in this manner the rest kept off. Having but little ammunition left, we were as sparing of it as possible; besides which we did not wish to irritate the natives more than they already were by firing, except when driven to it by necessity.

From our elevated situation we had a clear view of the landing-place, the boats at anchor waiting our return, the two canoes, and the ship. This we had but little prospect of ever again rejoining, though I had some hopes that Captain Robson would make an effort to rescue us, by arming himself, six Indian soldiers that were on board, two or three Europeans, and the people from the canoes. These hopes soon vanished, when I saw the canoes set sail and steer towards their island without passing alongside the ship.

The plain which surrounded the rock was covered with the armed savages assembled from all parts of the coast, amounting to several thousands, who had been in ambush waiting for us to land. This assemblage now exhibited a scene revolting to human nature. Fires were prepared and ovens heated for the reception of the bodies of our ill-fated companions, who, as well as the allied chiefs and their slaughtered men, were brought to the fires in the following manner. Two of the Vilear party placed a stick or a limb of a tree onto their shoulders, over which were thrown the bodies of their victims, with their legs hanging downwards on one side and their hands at the other. They were thus carried in triumph to the ovens prepared to receive them. Here they were placed in a sitting posture, while the savages sung and danced with joy over their prizes, and fired several musket-balls through each of the corpses, all the muskets of the slain having fallen into their hands.

As Thomas Daphne was wounded, Dillon told him to go down the rock, walk to the boat, and tell Captain Robson to release the prisoners in an exchange which might save the lives of the remaining white men. Daphne descended and, with Dillon covering him with his musket, reached the boat. Ten minutes later Daphne went aboard the ship.

Charles Savage now decided to go off the rock and talk with the natives. The Chinese, Luis, went down the other side of the rock to attempt a truce with the chief. Suddenly the natives gave a yell, grabbed Savage, and suspended him head down in a trough of fresh water until he drowned. Another savage stole up behind Luis and swung his club to crush the Chinese's skull.

Dillon later reported:

We, the three defenders of the hill, were then furiously attacked on all sides by the cannibals, whom our muskets however kept in great dread, though the chiefs stimulated their men to ascend and bring us down, promising to confer the greatest honours on the man who should kill me, and frequently inquired of their people if they were afraid of three white men, when they had killed several that day.

Thus encouraged, they pressed close on us. Having four

muskets between three of us, two always remained loaded: for Wilson being a bad shot, we kept him loading the muskets, while Martin Bushart and I fired them off. Bushart had been a rifleman in his own country, and was an excellent marksman. He shot twenty-seven of the cannibals with twenty-eight discharges only missing once: I also killed and wounded a few of them in self-defence. Finding they could not conquer us without a great sacrifice on their part, they kept off and vowed vengeance.*

As the three survivors watched from the top of the rock, the human bodies were brought out of the oven and given out to the different tribes. The chieftain now called up to Dillon, asking him to come down and be killed so that they could see to cut him up before darkness prevented accurate dissection. Dillon decided not to take advantage of the opportunity and told the savages that he was arranging for the release of eight native prisoners aboard the boat, who had been captured several days before. Finally the three survivors on the rock had only seventeen cartridges between them. They decided to shoot themselves to avoid the danger of falling into the hands of the cannibals. At the very moment when they agreed to shoot themselves simultaneously, Dillon noticed that the boat was put off from the ship. Soon it arrived at the landing place with the eight cannibal prisoners aboard.

Brought up to the rock along with a chest of cutlery and ironmongery, the eight prisoners were then bartered for in a truce agreement. Finally the natives agreed to allow the

* Chevalier Captain Pierre Dillon, *Narrative and Successful Result of a Voyage . . . To Ascertain the Actual Fate of La Pérouse's Expedition,* 1829.

three survivors to return to their boat in return for the eight
men, the cutlery and the ironmongery. Dillon and his men
then walked unmolested to the ship's boat.

Nevertheless, another crisis developed when the time came
to push the boat out into deep water. One of the natives
decided to make trouble and started after them. The three
men walked backward up to their breasts in water, climbed
aboard, and then started to row to the ship. A shower of
arrows and stones followed them, but they reached the ship
safely. The natives and the white people who did not want
to return to civilization were put ashore a few days later at
another island, Tucopia, where the natives were still friendly.
When Martin Bushart went ashore that was the last that
Mate Dillon saw of him for some years. Dillon's comments
follow:

From the year 1813 to May 1826 I heard nothing of
Martin Bushart. On my way then from Valparaiso and New
Zealand towards Bengal, I came in sight of Tucopia on the
morning of the 13th May, and shortly after several canoes
put off from the shore and pulled towards the ship. In the
foremost of them I recognized the lascar Joe, and invited
him on board. He had not the most distant recollection of
me until I made myself known to him, by saying I was the
captain of the cutter which brought him from the Beetee
Islands and landed him on Tucopia with Martin Bushart. He
appeared to have forgot the East-Indian dialects, and could
not reply to me or my servants, three of whom were his coun-
trymen. His conversation was composed of a mixture of
Bengalese, English, the Beetee, and Tucopia dialects.

The next canoe that reached the ship had Martin Bushart
on board. Having invited him on deck, I found that he also

had lost all recollection of me: until I reminded him of our old acquaintance, and providential escape from Vilear. He then informed me that no ship had visited the island for the first eleven years after he landed there; but that about twenty months back a whaler came off the island, and whaled for one month, during which time he went on board and remained with her until she sailed for England. He also mentioned that a second whaler had passed the island about ten months back, he went on board in a canoe, and remained about twenty minutes, when she set sail and stood to the westward.

One of my officers informed me that the lascar Joe had sold my armourer the silver guard of a sword. I sent for it, and on inspection observed five cyphers on it, not one of which however I could make out. On inquiry of Martin Bushart how he came by it, he informed me that on his first arrival at Tucopia he saw in the possession of the natives several ship's iron bolts, chain-plates, axes, knives, china and glass beads, with the handle of a silver fork, and many other things. He at first supposed that a ship must have been cast away here, and that the islanders procured those things from her wreck, but upon learning the language about two years after he had landed on the island, he found out his mistake.

The natives then informed him, that those things which he had seen, with the sword-guard, had been brought in their canoes from a distant island, which they called Mannicolo [Vanikoro], and that two large ships, such as the *Hunter* was, had been wrecked there, when the old men now in Tucopia were boys, and that there yet remained at Mannicolo large quantities of the wrecks. The lascar confirmed this report, and said he had been there about six years back, and that he had seen and conversed with two old men who belonged to the ships.

A native of Tucopia was then called in, who had returned from thence not more than six or seven months; he said that he had resided at the island where the ships were wrecked for two years, on his last visit, and that there were several parts of the wreck to be yet found. From all these statements being delivered in the undesigning manner in which they were, I immediately came to the conclusion that the two ships wrecked must be those under the command of the far-famed and lamented Count de La Pérouse, as no other two European ships were lost or missing at so remote a period.

I inquired of the islanders if any ship had been at Mannicolo since the two in question had been lost there. They replied, no: that ships had been seen passing the island at a great distance, but never had any communication with the shore.

I was very short of provisions, but notwithstanding this I determined to proceed to Mannicolo, and with such means as were in my power, to rescue from the hands of the savages the two survivors, who I had not the least doubt were Frenchmen.

I begged of Martin Bushart and the lascar to accompany me. The lascar refused to go on the journey, but Martin and one of the Tucopians agreed.

Unfortunately the ship was becalmed for the next seven days and by that time was leaking badly. When Dillon discovered food was running low, he decided to abandon the search and sailed for Bengal, which he reached on August 30, 1826. By this time he was convinced that La Pérouse's expedition had perished at the island of Mannicolo and so informed the Bengal government.

On hearing of Dillon's discovery, the East India Company

decided to place a survey vessel, the *Research,* under Captain
Dillon's command with orders for him to search for evidence
of the two craft. The ship sailed out of Calcutta in January,
1827. Unfortunately Dillon could not get along with his
associates, and had a most unfortunate habit of provoking
almost everyone aboard. When the *Research* reached Tasmania, the craft's doctor went ashore and brought action
against his captain. Fined fifty pounds and sentenced to two
months in jail, Dillon managed to get out in a few days, and
the expedition started again. Unhappily, the chief officer
became unruly, the clerk absconded with money, and the
crew mutinied at Port Jackson. Nevertheless, Vanikoro was
sighted on September 7, and Dillon went ashore to retrieve
any articles which would prove beyond doubt that the *Boussole* and the *Astrolabe* had been wrecked there.

After carrying on an investigation with the natives, Captain Dillon was given important but unhappy news. The
natives said at first that the crew of one of the ships had been
drowned, but later admitted that sixty French skulls had
been hung up in the spirit house at Whanoo, and Dillon
realized that the Frenchmen had been massacred. On the
other hand, the men on the other ship which had landed on
the beach had been given special privileges because the officers, wearing cocked hats, were believed to be gods. The
cocked hats, the natives had been told, were actually part of
the heads of the men. Nevertheless, no survivors were ever
found anywhere.

Many stories were told them. One involved a canoe which
had drifted ashore with five white men aboard. Three of
them had died, but the other two were still alive. Old and

toothless, they had to pound up their betel in a wooden mortar so they could chew it more easily.

One native version of the disaster which befell the two craft seems to fit all the known facts. The man who told it stated that the first ship anchored at Whanoo and the second at Paicu. Caught in a terrible hurricane, both vessels were driven ashore. The craft at Whanoo was battered ashore on rocks where the natives attacked the sailors, and the white people fought back with cannon and musketry fire. Soon the ship began to go to pieces. The crew took to the boats, but as each craft reached shore, the sailors were massacred almost to a man.

Meanwhile, the other ship was pushed by the waves onto a sandy beach, but the sailors were more circumspect in their actions. When the natives came down and fired their arrows, the white men held up axes, beads, and other trinkets as peace offerings. Appreciating these conciliatory acts, the natives then became friendly and allowed the white people to stay on the island. Building a boat of wood from the wreck, the majority of the sailors sailed away, promising to return for their comrades. They never came back.

Dillon now began to collect relics from the two French ships. He acquired a ring made from a spoon, some glass beads, a piece of eight and other fragments of metal. Anchoring inside the reef, he obtained pegs, swivel guns, chain, an eighteen-pound cannon ball, and a carved plank decorated with the fleur-de-lis.*

Finally Dillon decided to return to the Hooghly River where the governor general authorized him to sail with the relics of France. There King Charles X made him a Chevalier

* Later identified as having been carved in the Brest dockyard.

of the Legion of Honor, paid all his expenses, and gave him a pension of 4,000 francs annually for life. When the relics reached France, one expedition survivor was still alive in France. He was the Vicomte de Lesseps, whom La Pérouse had left on Kamchatka with dispatches, and he positively identified the objects as having been from the ships.

Meanwhile Captain Dumont d'Urville of the French frigate *Astrolabe* (the same name as the craft which disappeared) started out from France to continue the French government's search. Reaching Hobart, d'Urville apparently was afraid of aggravating Dillon, for the *Astrolabe* did not stop at Fort Jackson where d'Urville would have met Dillon. Finally d'Urville reached Vanikoro. He sent the native divers down to recover several more relics and to find the exact location where one of the French ships had been sunk.*

There was a small area through which a canoe could get beyond the breakers. Down at the bottom, fifteen feet deep, d'Urville could see anchors, cannon balls, and other wreckage. He now authorized the erection of a small monument to the memory of the men who had perished there. D'Urville believed that La Pérouse was headed for Santa Cruz at the time of his disaster. Possibly the two craft were sailing at night when they ran into the terrible reef of Vanikoro, the existence of which was entirely unknown at the time. Probably the *Boussole* was sailing ahead and struck the shoals without being able to get off, while the second ship had time to bear up into the wind and sail toward the open sea.

Realizing that the *Boussole* was lost, the captain of the *Astrolabe* probably attempted to reach the inside of the reef

* Dumont d'Urville, *Bibliothèque Universelle des Voyage Autour du Monde*, pp. 188–368.

to pick up the survivors, and in doing so met the same fate. As d'Urville writes:

This was, we can have no doubt about it, the cause of the loss of the second vessel. The very appearance of the place where it remains suggests this opinion, for at first one would think to find there a passage between the reefs. It is, then, possible that the Frenchmen on the second ship tried to go through this opening to the inside of the shoals and they only realized their mistake when they were lost.

In the year 1938 three Frenchmen visited Vanikoro in a small cutter and spent a month investigating traces of the two ships wrecked almost a century and a half before. They were M. Broise, M. Martinet, and M. Klein. After finding nothing of either the *Boussole* or the *Astrolabe,* they put up a cross on rocks near the reef off the island, which is believed to be there still. A marble tablet was placed at the foot of the cross in 1959.

As the years have gone by many people have searched for the wrecks. Around the year 1950 a British trader named Fred Jones found a piece of eight dated 1784 that came from the wreck. In 1956 he gave it to Pierre Anthonioz. The French naval patrol vessel *Tiara* carried out research in the area in 1956, but bad weather prevented the discovery of anything of importance.

Pierre Anthonioz became interested in finding wreckage from the *Astrolabe* and visited the Bibliothèque Nationale in Paris to study the original maps made in 1828 by a Lieutenant Gression. On Monday, March 17, 1958, his expedition reached the anchorage and began a search of the passage.

In the next few days they uncovered four anchors lying head to foot, one on top of the other. Near the end of the third day they uncovered a cannon, but by the time the various articles had been brought to the surface, the weight was so great that their fifty-four foot vessel, the *Don Quijote,* was very low in the water and the diving stopped.

Unquestionably, the Pierre Anthonioz expedition discovered the wreck of the *Astrolabe.* The unsolved enigma of the two craft may be settled forever should the French government send out another expedition to conduct diving operations on the sea bottom off Vanikoro.

CHAPTER 4

The *Navigator*

The American brig *Navigator* sailed in 1787 from Baltimore bound for France with a cargo of tobacco and staves. She never reached port, or as far as is known never sighted land again. The name of her captain is not known for sure but is believed to have been John Soete or Sutling. Nine members of her crew of ten did not live to tell the details of how she was wrecked, and the tenth man, under strange circumstances, came ashore in a foreign land.

The story of this event attracted the attention of Jacob August Riis, the great American journalist and reformer.* Mr. Riis, who was born in the old town of Ribe, Denmark, in 1849, returned to visit his birthplace in the summer of 1893. Ribe, which was once the seat of the Danish kings, has many almost forgotten treasures, and Jacob Riis wanted to find in the attic of his father's house a strange box that he recalled rummaging in when he was a child.

* *The Century Magazine,* Volume LII, pp. 913–916.

The day he picked to climb up to the attic was a very rainy one. He found the box for which he searched and discovered inside it two canvases on stretchers. The box was so shaky that when Mr. Riis began to explore it, the container literally fell to pieces. He then discovered that the canvases were oil paintings, damaged by rats, but still in fairly good condition. He held them up in front of him and then recalled that they had been in his room thirty years before.

Now very old, the frames were dropping off, but their very age added to the regard in which the Riis family had held them as rare works of art. The two paintings were of what apparently was the same object, an old-time full-rigged ship carrying the Danish flag in a rough sea. There was a wreck in the foreground. One of the pictures showed a boat steered by an officer in a red coat. It was approaching the wreck, on the bowsprit of which sat a man lashed to the spar and imploring aid. In the other painting the man had been taken off, with the Danish ship under way again and the wreck sinking into the sea. One of the two masts of the wreck had fallen in the second picture.

The two paintings showed a drama of the sea, but what the story was Jacob Riis could not tell. On neither canvas was there a title or the name of the artist. He wrote:

It all came back to me—the long winter nights when the west wind tore at our bedroom window and howled about the gables, and we lay awake listening for the voice of the bell in the old gray tower of the Dom. When the storm shook the tower to its foundations, the big bell gave forth a moan that sobbed through the night, filling it with a nameless dread.

We children pulled the bedclothes over our heads when we heard it above the smashing of roof-tiles on the cobblestones, and the watchman's warning cry that the sea was "coming in," and tried to think of the prayer for those "in danger of the deep" that kept company in the back of our prayer book with the petition against the wicked Turk, and the rest of the plagues of seafaring mankind.

On such nights, when the house shook in the blast so that we got up and lighted our candle at the peat fire for company, the old paintings had a weird fascination for me. In the flickering light of the tallow dip, dark shadows came and went upon them, and the cabin windows of the big ship shone as if lights were burning within; the sea heaved, threatening each moment to engulf the lone sailor on the bowsprit.

I knew their story then by heart. It had been told to me a hundred times, and it got to be so woven in with the storm and the danger in my thoughts that when, in the morning, I arose to find our town, set ordinarily in a landscape of smiling meadows, the center of a raging flood, fish jumping in the streets where we walked but yesterday, and drowned cattle lining the causeway, I half expected to see them lying there, ship, wreck, and all, right at our door.

Jacob Riis, thinking of the old memories, brought the paintings to his father and asked him about them, but he could tell his son nothing more than that they had been given to him nearly fifty years before by a minister of a nearby country church, who had been dead for many years.

In 1893, at the time of the rainy day visit to the attic, the preacher's son was then the dean of the *dom,* and Jacob Riis went to the dean in search of further information. Pastor Koch, who had been Riis's teacher in the Latin school, re-

membered the paintings, but could not tell how long they
had been in his family.

Later Jacob Riis came across something on the back of one
of the paintings that seemed to be a patch put over a tear in
the canvas. Closer inspection, however, showed traces of pen-
manship, and then gradually he found out that the writing
was a description of the wreck itself. With the help of a mag-
nifying glass, and after many hours of patient work, the
following inscription was deciphered:

View of wreck seen in the Spanish Sea, Januarii 7, 1788,
by the entire crew of the Royal Danish East India Company's
ship *Princess Charlotte Amalia.* It was an American brig, on
which sat a man lashed to the bowsprit, and was rescued by
the said Danish ship; they had been ten men in all, commanded by Captain Sutling, from Baldemore, in North
American, bound for Lorient, in France, with 75 Hogsheads
of tobacco and some staves; wrecked Januarii 7, and had since
preserfed life by means of tobacco. . . . The said sailor's name
was Dinnes Martin, who went with an American from Cape
Bonae Spei.

Drawn by the master of same

The name which had been signed to the painting had entirely disappeared. Riis applied chemicals to the painting,
and the name appeared with such sudden and brief distinct-
ness that Riis was thrown off his guard, and nearly lost it.
It was either Simon, or Limon. Nevertheless, it was not the
master of the *Charlotte Amalia* in which Riis was interested.
His goal was to learn the name of the master of the wrecked
and yet nameless ship.

It seemed strange that in an account written by a sailor the name of the wrecked vessel, which he must have known from the rescued man, should have been omitted. Jacob Riis, a reporter at the time, was considerably bothered by the fact that the name of the ship was so hopelessly missing.

His reporting instinct was aroused, and he decided to find out the last of this tragedy that had so fascinated him in his boyhood. He was beginning to be superstitious about it. His crossing the ocean and settling, as it were, in the very home of the century-old secret, and returning to find the paintings in the way he did, as if they had been waiting all the time for him—it all seemed to him a kind of providence. Nevertheless, he packed the old canvases in his trunk out of sight, and they traveled back with him to America.

On arriving in the United States he wrote to the collector of the Port of Baltimore, asking what vessel commanded by Captain Sutling cleared for Lorient in November or December, 1787, with such a cargo. The collector referred the inquiry to the keeper of records, who, after a careful search, found no trace of the ship.

The records of the period around 1787 were imperfectly kept, the keeper of the records wrote, and most of them had been destroyed by fire. Those that remained gave no clue.

At Washington Jacob Riis received no more encouragement. Next he tried Lloyd's of London, only to be told that the particulars he sought were past finding out. He was referred to the files of the Shipping List; but the thing he sought, the craft's name, was essential for using those. At this stage he gave up the sea and turned to the land. He searched the directories of every large city from Baltimore to San Francisco, but found no such name as Sutling there.

Riis was on the point of admitting defeat, when it occurred to him to go back to Denmark, where the paintings came from, for the rest of their half-told story. Jacob Riis now wrote an account of his investigations for a Danish paper, asking for help.

In a very few days it came from an unexpected source. The keeper of the government archives wrote that Riis's request seemed as if put directly and personally to him, since he was just then engaged in indexing the remnants of the papers pertaining to the great trading companies of the pre-Napoleonic era. He actually had before him, when he read the Riis appeal, the log of the *Princess Charlotte Amalia*, of the Royal Asiatic (or East India) Company's fleet, of the very voyage to China on which the adventure in the Spanish sea befell.

Under the date of January 7, 1788, the archivist found the following entry, made by "second fourth watch, under sail between Junloe and Porto Pray":

At eight o'clock sighted mast of a ship in southeast, about four miles away, but could see nothing of the hull. Saw what looked like efforts to signal, and signs of life on board, and braced away S.E. and E.S.E. down to the wreck, to see if there was anybody to save.

Got alongside at 10:30 and saw the wreck of a small vessel that had lost its foremast and maintopmast, which dragged alongside. . . . The hull was under water. A living man sat yet on the bowsprit. Hove to, and sent out the small boat in charge of mate, Helsting [the man in the red coat consequently], to take off the man. He boarded it, and reported that it was the brig *Navigator*, from Baldemode, in North America, Captain Suitzing, with a cargo of seventy-five hogsheads of tobacco, and some staves, consigned to Laurent, in France.

Had left Baldemode December 4, the year before. In the afternoon at four o'clock, as he ran before a stiff northwester with reefed foresail, the tiller broke, and, as the brig ran in the wind, it capsized on the instant. Of the crew of ten only the one man, Danis Market, was saved. He had sat on the bowsprit four days, without food or drink.

In the ship's protocol, kept by the supercargo, the rescued sailor is called Dinnes Martin, and the captain John Soete, and in a letter to the company's officials the captain of the *Charlotte Amalia* calls the sailor Dani Martin. No doubt his name was Dennis.

The purser's books show that he was well cared for. From the company's stores he was fitted out with "one flannel shirt, two pairs of stockings, two shirts, one pair of cloth trousers, and a pair of shoes." By January 10 Dennis had fully recovered, and was enrolled by his own wish in the ship's crew. On April 7 he left the ship at Cape Town by permission.

The artist's name is not disclosed by the record. There were four "masters" on board, but the name of none of them can be identified with Simon or Limon, unless it might be that of the Hovmester, Jansen.

And so it was that journalist Riis had several questions answered and knew at last the story of the two paintings, only to find other more urgent questions rising to take the place of those that had been answered. Had the old paintings kept their secret for Riis alone all these years, and why for him? Was the fate of the *Navigator* ever made known to those waiting for news of the lost ship at home? Did Dennis Martin ever return to tell the story of the wreck of the *Navigator?*

He "went with an American" from the Cape of Good Hope, said the long-hidden inscription. The *Charlotte Amalia*'s log said simply that he left the ship. Unless he himself brought news of the *Navigator*, it was certainly never heard of in the United States.

News traveled slowly in those times, and unhappy days followed quickly. For a quarter of a century after, the sea was not a safe highway for any but armed craft. When, at length, Napoleon was on St. Helena and peace restored to the world, the *Navigator* was long forgotten, and its owners, and all who belonged to its ill-fated captain and crew, were perhaps dead. The average sailor does not write letters. It was not the business of the Royal Asiatic Company to find the *Navigator*'s owners, and there is no evidence that it tried.

Suppose the mystery was never solved? May there not be living, then, to this day someone to whom the proof of the old paintings might mean restoration of lost property, the establishment of long-denied rights? Was Jacob Riis the custodian of the lost ship's secret that might right a century-old wrong by restoring the paintings to those who had a better claim upon them than Riis? Who can answer these questions? And where are the paintings today?

Jacob August Riis died on May 26, 1914, and the mystery of what became of Dennis Martin is still an unsolved enigma.

CHAPTER 5

Maine Treasure Hoards

During the many tours which I have made along the Maine coast I have gathered together scores of stories concerning the various hoards which have been the objectives of enthusiastic treasure hunters, searches which at times have approached the frenzied state.

Several of the hunts for Maine treasure have been successful, and quite a few caches of treasure have been found. In other books I have told of the Castine hoard, the Richmond's Island treasure, the Jewell Island gold pieces, and the treasure in a kettle found on Cedar Ledges near Two Bush Island, Casco Bay. Nevertheless, for every hoard discovered, there are scores which probably will lie buried for centuries to come. It is about several of the mysterious, unfound caches that I write in this chapter. Without question, because of improved methods of search, it is entirely within the realm of possibility that many elusive treasure hoards may be discovered within the next few years.

One story I enjoyed uncovering concerned digging for the treasure from a Spanish galleon, bounty which was unloaded at the so-called Bull's-eye Rock, near Cape Jellison, Maine. It was in this general vicinity that lighthouse keeper John Odum * of Fort Point Light was kidnapped with his son, Sidney, when they were sailing off Sandy Point in Stockton, near where the pirates planned to anchor and take treasure ashore. These came kidnappers were believed to have buried gold from a Spanish galleon in Stockton. The exact location, rumor has it, was at French's Point.

Even before Edgar Heath and his wife searched for the galleon treasure at French's Point, Edgar's father was said to have located a large metal treasure chest on Long Island. Unfortunately, Heath was digging alone. When his pick hit the top of the chest he realized that he could not move it by himself. He covered the chest with a few inches of soil, and returned three days later with a friend. Landing on the shore, they went at once to the location, but found that the cavity was three feet deeper than when Heath had left it. The treasure chest was gone!

Treasure-seeker Heath decided that he must have been observed the day that he found the chest. He reasoned that when he left the island those who had watched him, and there must have been several, went to the hole and dug out the treasure. Taking it off the island, they probably went ashore on the mainland with it. He never found out anything more about it, and to this day the mystery is unsolved.

I have never believed in divining rods for finding gold, but so many stories have been written about them that they

* Appointed April 8, 1853, to succeed William Cleuly, in service since September 8, 1836.

cannot be ignored. Those I have seen in Maine are strange-looking instruments. One I examined had a small glass tube at the top which was filled with iron filings. The top and bottom of the tube were secured with brass knobs, with two flexible rattan arms extending from below the knobs. Darius Bowden, who started the Heath family treasure hunting, tried out the rod in every location where gold or silver might have been buried in the general area of Fort Point Cove, but had no luck. Much of his efforts were in the vicinity of Bull's-eye Rock, so-called because two large glass eyes resembling those of a bull had been fitted into the rock by unknown people. When the sun or a bright moon reflected on the glass the result was uncanny.

There were the usual number of superstitious persons who would not go near the rock after dark because they claimed to have heard groans or other strange, fearsome noises in the area. Of course, the oft-told pirate stories were repeated—that when the buccaneers buried gold they killed one of their number and placed him alongside the chest so that his spirit might guard the treasure from being found by unqualified seekers. Years ago the glass bull's-eyes were removed from the rock, also by unknown people, but one can still see the sockets in which the eyes were set. Many believe that pirates fitted the eyes in the rock to mark the spot where they had buried treasure.

Darius Bowden transferred his treasure-hunting activities to French's Point shortly after the brief kidnapping of the two Odums became known. Bowden's son-in-law, Edgar Heath, told how experiments were carried out, but admitted there was no find of treasure.

Edgar's father often experimented with the divining rod

on many islands in Penobscot Bay and also on the mainland.
He did a lot of fishing off Gott's Island, and one day on an
island not far from Gott's they used the rod and were greatly
excited when the instrument showed attraction. They dug
a large hole without finding a trace of anything, and the next
day at dawn they started again for the island to resume their
digging, when they saw a strange schooner drop anchor
nearby.

Watching with great attention, they noticed sailors lower
an aged, bearded man to a boat which was rowed ashore.
Upon reaching the shore the old man was taken to a log,
where he sat down. From that position he pointed to a certain spot. Three sailors started digging where Edgar's father
had dug. Heath and his companions were outnumbered and
realized the visitors were pirates, or at least the old man had
been one, and would not allow interruption. After an hour's
digging the visitors found the treasure, after which everyone
departed for the boat, which soon sailed away. Heath and his
two friends landed on the island, where they found that the
sailors had dug only two feet deeper in the same hole to get
the hoard. At the bottom was the imprint of an iron chest,
with patches of rust.

Heath again used the divining rod over the rust, but there
was no longer any attraction. He always believed that the
old man was the sole survivor of an ancient pirate band that
had utilized the small island to cache the treasure.

Darius Bowden gave Mr. and Mrs. Edgar Heath their first
lessons in handling the divining rod. Very superstitious,
Bowden often claimed he heard groans while digging for
treasure. One night two spiritualists, one named Porter and
the other Mack, asked Heath to take the divining rod and

go with them to French's Point, where they hoped to locate the gold supposed to have been buried by the pirates who kidnapped the lighthouse keeper and his son. They asked Heath not to run if any strange noises were heard.

Mrs. Heath went along with the party. The rod showed plenty of attraction for a certain spot on the point, and they started digging. They had gone down about two feet when a noise was heard. Heath kept right on digging but the two spiritualists fled. However, no treasure was found.

The divining rod always showed a strong attraction at French's Point and also around Bull's-eye Rock. Local residents at Cape Jellison always insist that many pirates visited the area. It was an excellent place for a hideout, and there were many islands and coves where they could careen their vessels.

The story of Captain Tom Shute was told to me once by Henry Buxton, author of *Assignment Down East*. Tom was captured by pirates at the mouth of the bay, and when brought aboard the ship he found the pirate captain was an old schoolmate of his on Verona Island. The pirate freed Shute after the latter had promised that he would never reveal the Verona Islander's identity. Although Captain Shute kept his promise, many were sure that the islander's name was Lord.

I have often written of the notorious pirate whose name was Captain Gibbs. Many State of Mainers claim he frequently visited Penobscot Bay. Charles Gibbs was born on his father's Rhode Island farm in 1794. Committing acts of outrageous nature in the community, he was told by his father to reform, but instead Charles ran away and became a pirate at the age of fifteen.

Several years later he was forced to bury a treasure on Pelican Island, New York, and then left for another siege of freebooting. Captain Gibbs sailed up the Penobscot River, put into the south branch of the Marsh River, and replenished his depleted stores with vegetables, meats, and other supplies from the nearby farms of Frankfort settlers. According to the natives he never harmed the settlers, and they were always glad to see his ship sail in because he paid generously for his supplies in gold. He was a swaggering, blustering fellow, and his vessel was manned by a villainous crew of ruffians.

Whenever Gibbs visited the Penobscot River area, he always anchored in the south branch of the Marsh River within a few yards of a great gravel mound, which at that time is said to have been 100 feet in height. One day in 1946 I visited Frankfort, where my grandfather, Joshua, was born in 1837, but no one to whom I talked seemed to know of the gravel mound. There seems to have been no geological reason for the presence of this mound in this otherwise flat salt marsh. Possibly it was left there by a sliding glacier in the long ago ice age, or centuries ago it might have been erected by the Indians as a burial place.

It is likely that the settlers started digging in the mound soon after they heard that Gibbs had been hanged on the New York gallows on Friday, April 22, 1831. Of course, the usual rumors were circulated that he had buried a great chest of gold and jewels in the Frankfort mound. These rumors of treasure-trove have persisted down through the years, each generation of Frankfort folk, and many outsiders, too, taking a hearty turn with picks, crowbars, and shovels at the old mound. As the years went by, the mound dwindled under the repeated attacks of picks and shovels wielded by treasure seekers. Tons and tons of gravel were dug away and thrown on the flat surface of the marsh, where the river soon carried it away.

During my visit to Frankfort in 1946 I spent some time attempting to locate the mound by myself, but failed completely. I did find a cemetery which was allowed to go to ruin, the trees growing right up through the graves and the gravestones, but I decided that the generation which knew of the mound had all passed on, and their descendants in Frankfort knew nothing of this mystery.

CHAPTER 6

La Lutine

One of the great unsolved mysteries in the world is what has become of the $3,000,000 in gold and silver within the sunken hulk of the British frigate *La Lutine* at the bottom of the sea off the Zuider Zee in Holland.

From the year 1914, when I first read of this treasure, I have been gathering material on the history of the vessel and the many attempts to salvage its hoard of wealth.

About twenty years ago, while in England, I was finally able to carry out what at that time was one of my fondest dreams. Visiting Lloyd's of London, I was able to see for myself the bell of the *La Lutine* and the table and chair made from material recovered in early *La Lutine* salvage attempts.

On March 30, 1963, I received a communication from the secretary of Lloyd's Register of Shipping that answered my final questions. In addition the letter contained a substantial documental history of the old frigate and her cargo of silver and gold, which added several items to my store of knowledge concerning the famous frigate.

The *La Lutine* was launched in France for the French navy in 1785. Captured by the British at Toulon in 1793, she was re-equipped as a thirty-two-gun frigate and commissioned in the British fleet. In October, 1799, an application was made by merchants to Lord Duncan, commanding admiral in the North Sea, for a King's ship to carry gold and silver to Hamburg "because there was no packet for that purpose." The total amount originally on board the *La Lutine* is unknown, but its value has been placed as high as $5,000,000. Most of this valuable cargo was insured at Lloyd's.

On the ninth of October, 1799, *La Lutine* sailed from Yarmouth Roads for Hamburg. During the night of the ninth and tenth of October, 1799, she was wrecked between the islands of Vlieland and Terschelling off the north coast of Holland.

Since that date efforts have been made from time to time to recover the treasure on board, and gold and silver bars and coins have been salved by various ingenious means. Just prior to World War II a dredger brought up one gold bar, a few coins, some cannon balls, and several pieces of timber. Other items salvaged from time to time included a portion of the log slate, a hammer, the stock of a pistol, three guns, some grapeshot, a rusted watch, a rusted penknife, a portion of a clay pipe, and the vessel's rudder. The last has been cut up and rebuilt into a table and a chair which now stand in the writing room at Lloyd's and are used by the chairman when addressing members. Lloyd's has never released its claim on the wealth from *La Lutine* still at the bottom of the sea.

The bell was recovered during the course of one of the

more successful salvage attempts in 1859. It hangs on the
rostrum in the underwriting room at Lloyd's and is rung
to call the attention of members when an important announcement is to be made, at which time one stroke means
that bad news is to follow and two strokes good news. In the
old days the bell normally indicated news of an overdue
vessel, but in these days of improved navigational aids overdue vessels are few, although on July 8, 1958, and October
29, 1959, the bell was rung twice to report the safe arrival
of "overdues."

The bell is also rung on important social occasions such
as when Her Majesty the Queen came to Lloyd's in November, 1952, to lay the foundation stone of the new building
and when the building was opened by Her Majesty Queen
Elizabeth, the Queen Mother, on November 14, 1957. At
each visit the bell was rung twice. The bell weighs 106
pounds and is $17\frac{1}{2}$ inches in diameter.

The history of this gigantic insurance organization goes
back to the days of Queen Anne. More than a quarter-mil-
lenium ago Edward Lloyd kept a coffeehouse in Tower
Street, London. Lloyd's became a popular meeting place for
underwriters, insurance brokers, and sea captains who needed
a gathering place to discuss new ships in port, wrecks, and
ships which were missing. In time the popular coffeehouse
became recognized as an unofficial headquarters for maritime
insurance speculation.

In 1773 this loosely organized business for ship insurance
matters took a great step forward by moving bodily into the
Royal Exchange, and from then on was known as Lloyd's.
From this unusual beginning, the present-day Lloyd's of
London was created.

The arrival book and the loss book at Lloyd's post move-
ments of vessels all over the world, and every wreck (there is
an average of more than two a day) is listed. The oldest
policy in the world involving maritime insurance is still on
exhibition at Lloyd's. A faded document which was issued
January 20, 1680, it covers the insurance of 1,200 pounds
on the vessel *Golden Fleece* sailing from Lisbon to Venice.

Silver plates on both the table and armchair made from
the *La Lutine's* wood read as follows:

H.B.M. Ship La Lutine
32 Gun Frigate
Commanded by Captain Lancelot Skynner, R.N.
Sailed from Yarmouth Roads
On the morning of the 9th October, 1799 with a large
amount of specie on board
And was wrecked off the Island of Vlieland the same night,
When all on board were lost except one man.*

Although Lloyd's still owns the frigate on the bottom of
the sea, the organization has not collected a shilling on her
since 1938.

In 1910 Captain E. F. Inglefield, an investigator, stated
that various attempts had already been made with the permission of Lloyd's to recover the treasure, but no real results
were apparent until 1886 when steam suction dredges were
first used. In that year, in addition to 700 pounds of gold
and silver coins, two guns were brought up from the wreck,
one of which was presented by Lloyd's to the Corporation
of London and is now on exhibition in the museum at the

* This man is said to have died on his way back to England.

Guild Hall. In 1891 more coins were recovered. Five years later another cannon was brought up.

An article which appeared in 1911 in Lloyd's weekly newspaper describes a new method of the period for raising sunken wealth:

An extraordinary machine was towed to the mouth of the River Colne, off Brightlingsen, and anchored on Thursday. It is to be used in a final attempt to recover 500,000 pounds treasure of gold, in coins and bars, which is said to have gone down in H.M.S. *Lutine* in 1797 near the island of Terschelling, off the coast of Holland.

A portion of the treasure has been recovered, but the ordinary dredging plant is now useless, as the vessel has sunk into the sand. The new device is a great steel tube nearly 100 ft. in length, and wide enough to allow a man to walk erect down its centre. At one end is a metal chamber provided with windows and doors, and at the other a medley of giant hooks and other tackle.

The apparatus has just been completed, after years of work, by Messrs. Forrest and Co., shipbuilders, in their Wyvenhoe yard. One end of the tube, it is explained, will be clamped to the side of a steamship or barge. The other end, by means of water ballast tanks, will be sunk until it touches the bottom. Then, by means of compressed air, all the water will be forced from the tube and also from the chamber at the bottom of it, which will be flush upon the bed of the sea.

Divers will walk down a stairway in the centre of the tube until they reach the submerged chamber. Here they will don their diving costumes, and, opening a series of water tight doors, will step out into the water. Engineers will be stationed in the chamber, and, following the instructions of the divers, who will communicate with them by means of portable telephones, they will operate the mechanism of two powerful suction pumps, or dredges, which are fitted to the sides of the tube.

These dredges, it is hoped, will suck away the sand around the sides of the heavy chamber until it gradually sinks by its own weight right down on to the deck of the wrecked ship. Then the divers, making their way from the chamber to the deck of the ship, and thence to the hold, will be able to transfer the treasure from the ship to the chamber by easy stages.

The best contemporary account of the loss of the *La Lutine* appeared on October 19, 1799, when the *Gentleman's Magazine* of London * published the following:

Intelligence was this day received at the Admiralty from Admiral Mitchell, communicating the total loss of *La Lutine,* of 32 guns, Captain Skynner, on the outward bank of the Fly Island Passage, on the night of the 9th inst., in a heavy gale at N.N.W. *La Lutine* had, on the same morning, sailed from Yarmouth Roads with several passengers, and an immense quantity of treasure for the Texel; but a strong lee-tide rendered every effort of Captain Skynner to avoid the threatened danger unavailable, and it was alike impossible during the night to receive any assistance, either from the *Arrow,* Captain Portlock, which was in company, or from the shore, from whence several [craft] were in readiness to go to her. When the dawn broke, *La Lutine* was in vain looked for; she had gone to pieces, and all on board unfortunately perished, except two men who were picked up, and one of

* The Harvard College Library has a copy.

whom has since died from the fatigue he has encountered.
The survivor is Mr. Shabrack * a notary public. In the annals of our naval history there has scarcely ever happened a
loss attended with so much calamity, both of a public as well
as a private nature.

There are several unsolved mysteries concerning the sailing of the *La Lutine*. The first is that in almost every account of the *La Lutine* wreck, it is stated that the frigate was
bound to the Texel and that the treasure she carried was to
pay off the British forces in Holland. There is no foundation
for either statement in fact. Actually the *La Lutine* was
headed for the river Elbe and Hamburg, and the treasure
was owned by London merchants who were connected with
Lloyd's. Therefore it was purely a commercial venture. It is
also an unsolved mystery as to how an experienced officer
drove his ship onto the dangerous shoals off the Zuider Zee.

Still another unsolved enigma of the *La Lutine* is how this
thirty-two-gun frigate of the Royal Navy was working as a
packet, carrying cargo for private individuals. When it is
realized that the total value of the gold and silver aboard
represented the equivalent of more than $3,000,000, we can
get some idea of the magnitude of the enterprise.

Without question, Admiral Lord Duncan was one of the
chief actors in the scheme to use government vessels in
private enterprise. I am in possession of a copy of Admiral
Duncan's letter of October 9, 1799, written to the British
Admiralty. An excerpt follows:

* This, of course, does not agree with the statement the secretary of
Lloyd's wrote to me stating that there were no survivors.

The merchants interested in making remittances to the continent for the support of their credit, having made application to me for a King's ship to carry over a considerable sum of money, on account of there being no Packet for that purpose, I have complied with their request, and ordered the *Lutine* to Cuxhaven with the same, together with the mails lying there for want of conveyance; directing Captain Skynner to proceed to Stromness immediately after doing so, to take under his protection the Hudson's Bay ships and see them in safety to the Nore.

Actually, before the letter reached the Admiralty the frigate and the treasure were at the bottom of the sea on the sunken sand banks of Holland.

The question might be asked at this late date as to why Admiral Duncan was not censured for this disaster. The answer is that the merchants of London and Lloyd's were powerful enough not only to hire ships of the British Navy, but to suppress public complaints if tragedy followed. It is paradoxical that the *La Lutine,* loaded with gold owned by Lloyd's of London and insured by them, went down in as serious a shipping disaster as took place anywhere in the world in that period.

Possibly a word or two might be said about the Zuider Zee, off which the *La Lutine* met her fate. Around the edge of the Zuider Zee was land where farmers grew their produce until the thirteenth century when a great storm cut through Holland. A second inlet appeared in 1287 as the result of another hurricane which took 100,000 lives. Ever since then the channels and the shoals have been shifting until what was once the coastline is now a confusion of islands and sand banks.

Upon hearing of the *La Lutine*'s disaster, salvage-minded Lloyd's promptly dispatched agents to the scene of the wreck. Most of the coin had been insured, and the loss was paid in full within two weeks of the disaster. Another gigantic sum of money was shipped shortly afterward to the original destination and reached Hamburg without any trouble.

The Netherlands government now claimed the *La Lutine* as a prize of war because England and Holland were engaged at that time in a halfhearted conflict. Lloyd's therefore could not attempt to find the treasure at once, and the Dutch fishermen in the area reaped a golden harvest, recovering treasure worth 83,000 pounds sterling in eighteen months. A list of what they recovered has been preserved:

    41,697 Spanish silver pistoles
        58 bars of gold, weight 646 lbs. 23 ounces
        35 bars of silver, weight 1,758 lbs. 8 ounces
         4 English guineas
       179 Spanish gold pistoles
        81 double Louis d'or
       138 single Louis d'or

Finally in December, 1801, the fishermen stopped their work, believing that they had found all the treasure. It was not long, however, before legends began to spring up about the golden wreck.

After Napoleon had been sent to isolation on St. Helena, Pierre Eschauzier, holding the post of Upper Strand Finder,*

---

* This unusual title meant that Eschauzier was entitled to make a business of salvage work in his area.

became vitally interested in the wreck. Holland granted him money enough to equip an expedition, but when he arrived on the scene he found that the wreck had sunk deep into the quicksands. Nevertheless he tried for seven years and found only a few gold coins. A diving bell was then put into use and it also failed.

Lloyd's of London, hearing of the expedition, announced that Holland did not own the wreck and had no claim on it. On May 6, 1823, the Secretary of the English Foreign Office, F. Conyngham, stated that after much negotiation:

His Netherlands' Majesty has expressed his willingness to cede to the British claimants the whole of that moiety of the said property which by His Netherlands' Majesty's decree of the 14th September, 1821, was reserved for the use of his said Majesty. The other moiety was, by the same decree, granted in the nature of salvage to a private company of his own subjects, who undertook to recover the cargo at their own expense. It has been stipulated that the British claimants shall be at liberty to concert with the said company as to the best mode of effecting that recovery. Considering the difficulties which the negotiation has experienced from disputed points of law, and making due allowance for the engagements formed with the Dutch company, who have been recognized as salvors by the Dutch law, and would have a right to have all services rewarded in the Courts of Holland for the property which may be saved by their exertions, Mr. Canning apprehends that it may be advisable for the claimants in this country to agree to the offer now made. The season for operation is now before them, and no hope could be reasonably entertained that a renewal of the negotiation would bring the matter to a more reasonable close.

Lloyd's of London finally agreed to accept a 50 per cent interest in its own wreck in case any diving group wished to conduct salvage on the *La Lutine*. For the next twenty-five years the *La Lutine* was left undisturbed. Then two divers from England named Hill and Downes petitioned the king of the Netherlands for permission to pick up as much gold as they could among the timbers of the wreck. The request was granted, with the provision that half of all that was found must be given to Lloyd's. The two divers did not appear at the wreck, but when the general public found out that individuals could dive there, the old Dutch company, founded by the Upper Strand Finder, opened negotiations. The Dutch company undertook to salvage the gold and agreed to pay over one-half to Lloyd's.

In 1857 Lloyd's received the following statement from its agent at the Texel:

I feel most happy to inform you that the new efforts to save the value out of the *Lutine* have not been without success. Yesterday there was recovered by means of divers and pincers, 13 silver coins, being Spanish piastres, 1 gold Louis d'or, 5 brass hoops and casks, and a quantity of cannon and shot.

Considering the value of the saved objects, it may not be of much signification; but the salvage itself is of very great importance, as it proves two facts, namely, first that the wreck of *La Lutine* has really been found, and secondly that there is specie still in the wreck. As soon as anything more is picked up, I will inform you immediately thereof. Be assured, I have taken the necessary steps to secure the interests of Lloyd's committee, as owners of the treasure, which we hope may entirely be saved.

When the word became general knowledge, the fishermen returned to the Zuider Zee and started dredging with their primitive instruments again. At one period there were sixty-eight large and well-manned boats in the immediate neighborhood looking for plunder.

Finally in 1861 the treasure seekers abandoned their work. A short time before that date a great gale out of the northwest had pushed the *La Lutine* deeper into the treacherous sands. However, Lloyd's received 22,162 pounds as the 50 per cent share in the salvage work before operations stopped.

In the year 1886 a resident of Bodegraven, Holland, Ter Meulen by name, was given permission to use a dredge on the *La Lutine* for the first time. He had been keeping a careful check on her location and between 1886 and 1889 recovered coins to the value of almost 687 English pounds.

In 1893 a new contract was signed by Lloyd's with W. R. Kinipple an Englishman. In the following year John Fletcher started with a suction dredge, but the sand filled the hole just as fast as the suction pump pulled it out. Nothing of importance resulted.

Shortly afterward Simon Lake of America became interested in the *La Lutine* and built a submarine recovery tube for the *Lutine* group, but again the results were not outstanding.

A new group now won the approval of Lloyd's to start salvage work and in November, 1910, began operations at the site. Their salvage vessel, the *Lyon,* operating with powerful pumps, brought up human bones, cannons, silver, and gold, but before real treasure in large amounts was encountered, World War I stopped operations.

In 1921 a new plan was put in effect, using a coal-grabbing machine, but the operators found less than a fathom of water over the site and were hampered in their activity. Nothing was recovered. Again in 1928 a new company was formed, but little of importance resulted from their efforts.

On July 26, 1933, an iron tower was set on the site. Great hopes were entertained for substantial treasure recovery, but the tower collapsed, having been built of fragile material. Another one erected in 1934 was found to be impractical.

The last professional visit to the location where the *La Lutine* is sinking deeper and deeper into the quicksands off the Zuider Zee was in 1938. The seagoing dredge *Karimata,* 246 feet long, with a breadth of 75.5 feet and drawing 10 feet, arrived on the scene.*

She began work on June 9. On July 29 she dredged up a gold bar weighing more than seven pounds. A silver watch with a lock of hair still inside was then removed from the silt, and many other items were recovered at this time. Before operations ended on September 12, in addition to the gold bar, 8 gold coins and 123 pieces of silver were found.

The exact amount of treasure remaining today is impossible to ascertain, as only part of the original cargo of gold and silver was insured and much unclassified gold coin and bullion arrived aboard the frigate a few hours before sailing. The Upper Strand Finder made an accounting which apparently is as close to the facts as we will ever get. These figures have been endorsed by John Mavor Hill, the Lloyd's agent at Amsterdam, and also accepted by the Dutch:

* Low tide surveys indicated that the depth was 13 feet.

Total salvage between 1800 and
   1861 . . . .   99,893 pounds sterling
Total treasure estimated to have
   been lost 1,175,000   "   "
Treasure remaining in the
   wreck 1,076,109   "   "

Thus the conservative person must assume that about $3,000,000 in gold and silver is still aboard the *La Lutine*. It is pleasing to know that at any moment the combination of a strong hurricane and the usual shifting currents in the vicinity may again expose in the water the bones of the frigate, with the gold bars also available to a diver. This romantic maritime insurance story has not been fully told yet, and I am confident that the unsolved mystery regarding the $3,000,000 in gold and silver bars, Spanish pistoles, and pieces of Louis d'or may sometime be a wonderful, complete tale of salvage.

CHAPTER 7

The Guns of Barisal

It seems a far cry from a lighthouse off the shores of Ostend, Belgium, to Great Falls, Montana. The subject of this chapter, unsolved, mysterious noises takes us to many other locations. My interest in Barisal guns began on September 19, 1958, when I took Averich Baruah, a resident of Assam, India, for a trip in my canoe in Marshfield, Massachusetts. It was then that he told me of the province of ten million inhabitants known as Assam and of strange, unaccountable noises in the general area.

Studying the history of Assam later, I discovered more details of what are generally called Barisal guns. Barisal is a town of India, between Calcutta and Assam. The *Encyclopaedia Britannica* tells us that Barisal, situated on a river of the same name, "has given its name to a curious physical phenomenon known as 'Barisal guns,' noises, like the report of a cannon which appear to come from the direction of the sea."

Actually, the term Barisal guns has grown to be identified with any strange unexplained noise in any part of the world resembling even vaguely the firing of guns or cannon. It is quite possible that the Barisal guns were not guns at all but sounds which resemble the firing of guns more than anything else. I now quote several statements concerning the Barisal guns, gleaning the accounts from many sources.*

In the year 1895 three men wrote of their interest in Barisal guns. M. van der Broeck, conservator of the Museum of Natural History of Belgium, stated that he had constantly noticed these sounds in the plain of Limburg since 1880, and his colleague of the Geological Survey, M. Rutot, had heard them very frequently along the Belgium coast:

The keeper of the lighthouse at Ostend has heard these noises for several years past; they are known near Boulogne, and the late M. Houseau spoke of them to my friend M. Lancaster. More than ten of my personal acquaintances have observed the fact.

The detonations are dull and distant, and are repeated a dozen times or more at irregular intervals. They are usually heard in the daytime when the sky is clear, and especially towards evening after a very hot day. The noise does not at all resemble artillery, blasting in mines, or the growling of distant thunder.

H. S. Olcott, of Madras, comments as follows:

I have read with interest *Nature* for October 31, on "The Barisal Guns." I refer to the *Theosophist* magazine for two

* *Nature* magazine of England is particularly rich in discussions of Barisal guns.

articles upon my personal observations at Barisal village itself, in the Gangetic delta. All the various theories until then propounded by men of science to account for the phenomenon in question were severally reviewed and pronounced inadequate. I have intended writing a third and final article, but found it impracticable. A writer in *Nature* is quite wrong in supposing that the sound of the "Barisal Gun" is "dull and distant," and that "it does not resemble artillery." However the like sounds may so seem to the Ostend lighthouse keeper, they were so sharp and loud that I thought the "evening gun" was being fired at a cantonment in the village and asked a friend standing by if that were so.

G. B. Scott, also writing to the same magazine, tells us that he first heard the guns in 1871 when he was traveling from Assam to Calcutta:

The weather was calm and clear, no sign of any storms. All day the noises on board the steamer prevented other sounds from being heard; but when all was silent at night, and we were moored in one or other of the narrow channels in the neighborhood of Barisal, Morelgunge, and upwards, far from any villages or other habitations, with miles and miles of long grass jungle on every side, the only sounds the lap of the water or the splash of earth, falling into the water along the banks, then at intervals, irregularly, would be heard the dull muffled boom as of distant cannon.

Sometimes a single report, at others two, three, or more in succession; never near, always distant, but not always equally distant. Sometimes the reports would resemble cannon from two rather widely separated opposing forces, at other times from different directions but apparently always from the southward, that is seaward.

We were not very far from the sea when I first heard them, and on mentioning to an old lady on board that I heard distant cannon, she first told me of the mysterious sounds known as the "Barisal Guns."

I specially remember spending a quiet Sunday, in the month of May, with a friend at Chilmari, near the river-bank. We had both remarked the reports the night before, and when near the hills previously. About 10 A.M. in the day, weather clear and calm, we were walking quietly up and down the river-bank, discussing the sounds, when we heard the booming distinctly, about as loud as heavy cannon would sound on a quiet day, about ten miles off, down the river. Shortly after we heard a heavy boom very much nearer, still south. Suddenly we heard two quick successive reports, more like horse-pistol or musket (not rifle) shots close by. I thought they sounded in the air about 150 yards due west of us over the water. My friend thought they sounded north of us. We ran to the bank, and asked our boatmen, moored below, if they heard them, and if so in what direction. They pointed south!

In the spring of 1865, on the southern slopes of the Himalayas, the report of a heavy gun was heard, clear and distinct, in the direction of the mountains near Buxa, Bhutan. A long way off, they were followed closely and at irregular intervals by other discharges. . . . Colonel Godwin Austen tells us that the reports were ". . . more like artillery fire than any I afterwards heard in the hills further to the east. These last had the nature of a very, very distant boom."

In *Nature*, May 7, 1896, Edward Fry writes as follows:

In the correspondence on this subject I have not noticed any reference to the noises said to be heard in the mountains of the peninsula of Sinai. In his *Sinai and Palestine* the late Dean Stanley refers to "the mysterious noises which have from time to time been heard on the summit of Jebel Musa, in the neighbourhood of Um Shaumer, and in the mountain of Makus or the Bell, so called from the legend that the sounds proceed from the bells of a convent enclosed within the mountain. In this last instance the sound is supposed to originate in the rush of sound down the mountain side. . . . In the case of Jebel Musa, where it is said that the monks had originally settled on the highest peak, but were by these strange noises driven down to their present seat in the valley, and in the case of Um Shaumer, where it was described by Burckhardt as like the sound of artillery, the precise cause has never been ascertained."

Burckhardt, in his *Travels in Syria and the Holy Land* refers to these noises and says: "The wind and weather are not believed to have any effect upon the sound."

In Palmer's *Desert of the Exodus,* the author tells of an Arab legend about a fairy maiden who fires off a gun one day in every year to give notice of her presence. Palmer believed that the noise is "in all probability caused by masses of rock becoming detached by the action of frost, and rolling with a mighty crash over the precipice [of 3,000 feet] into the valley below." The sounds at Jebel Nagus, which have also a legend connected with them, are undoubtedly due to the friction of rolling sand. From experiments made by the explorers, the degree of coarseness of the sand, the angle of inclination of the slope, and temperature seem to be the controlling conditions.

Similar noises have been heard at Dartmoor, England; in Scotland; and on the shores of Lough Neagh in Ireland.

Unusual explosion-like sounds have often been heard on the shores of Lough Neagh. Rev. W. W. Smith of Antrim writes in 1896:

When near the lake, I heard . . . cannon-like sounds. In time I came to understand that it was not from the opposite shores, but from the lake itself that the sounds proceeded. After questioning many of the local residents, I extended my enquiries to the fishermen, but they could assign no cause. A strange thing about the matter is that the people generally know nothing of the phenomenon, and that it is shrouded in mystery. . . . I have heard the sound probably twenty times during the present year, the last being on a Sunday afternoon a month since, when I heard two explosions; but with two exceptions they have all seemed to come many miles away, from different directions at different times. They have come apparently from Toome Bay, from the middle of the lake, and from Langford Lodge Point, about nine miles distant.

I have as yet spoken to no one who observed any movement of the waters when the explosions took place, nor have I spoken to any one who was close to the spot at the time, rather every one seems to have heard them only in the distance, which is strange, as fishermen are on the lake during many months in the year, at all hours of the day and night.

"Mist poeffers," or fog hiccups, are often heard off the Belgian coast and also have been reported from many parts of Australia. The earliest account of these which I can trace is that given by Captain Charles Sturt,* when describing his journey begun in 1828, at the time he discovered the Darling

* See *Two Expeditions into the Interior of Southern Australia*, 1834.

and Murray Rivers. Encamped near the Darling in February, 1829, he notes in his journal:

About 3 P.M. on the 7th, Mr. Hume and I were occupied tracing the chart upon the ground. The day had been remarkably fine, not a cloud was there in the heavens, nor a breath of air to be felt. On a sudden we heard what seemed to be the report of a gun fired at the distance of between five and six miles. It was not the hollow sound of an earthly explosion, or the sharp cracking noise of falling timber, but in every way resembled a discharge of a heavy piece of ordnance. On this all were agreed, but no one was certain whence the sound proceeded.

Both Mr. Hume and myself had been too attentive to our occupation to form a satisfactory opinion; but we both thought it came from the N.W. I sent one of the men immediately up a tree, but he observed nothing unusual. The country around him seemed to be equally flat on all sides, and to be thickly wooded; whatever occasioned the report, it made a strong impression on all of us; and to this day, the singularity of such a sound, in such a situation is a matter of mystery to me.

Years later, in 1928, I played football at Great Falls, Montana, for Intermountain College of Helena. While visiting the local library there I read the Lewis and Clark expedition journal, and discovered that on July 4, 1808, the Lewis and Clark expedition was encamped at Great Falls. Studying their journal, I learned that they also heard strange booming noises:

Since our arrival at the Falls we have repeatedly heard a strange noise coming from the mountains in a direction a little to the north of west. It is heard at different periods of the day and night, sometimes when the air is perfectly still and without a cloud, and consists of one stroke only, or five or six discharges in quick succession. It is loud, and resembles precisely the sound of a six-pound piece of ordnance at the distance of three miles.

Although I have been in Great Falls on several occasions since my first visit, on no occasion have I ever heard sounds even remotely resembling the sound of ordnance being fired, nor have I been able to talk with anyone who had.

An expedition sponsored by John Jacob Astor * was in the Black Hills of Wyoming and Dakota in 1810, and reported that in calm and serene weather, "and at all times of the day or night, successive reports are now and then heard among these mountains, resembling the discharge of several pieces of artillery. Similar reports were heard by Messrs. Lewis and Clark in the Rocky Mountains." Incidentally, in the year 1854, a man named Doty heard what he believed were like noises in the same vicinity, and he was certain that they came from the mountains. As far as is known, the sounds were never heard again.

Barisal guns have often been heard in Haiti, especially in the autumn and winter months.† There the sound is known as *gouffre*. Out at sea the Barisal guns have been heard on many occasions. An entry in the meteorological log of the S.S. *Resolute,* Captain W. Deuchars, for July 30, 1883, 8:00 P.M., reads as follows: "Six reports like those of guns heard to the westward, supposed to be caused by electricity,

---

* *Nature,* Volume III, 1896.
† The year 1912 was remembered for the many times the guns were heard.

as no ships are thought to be in the vicinity." The position is given as 71°09′ N., 12°28′ W., about sixty miles westward of Jan Mayen Island in the North Atlantic Ocean.

Many explanations have been suggested—fireworks, actual gunfire, thunderclaps, the collapsing of banks and submarine eruptions—but so far none of these has been accepted by those who have heard the sounds.

Lieutenant Colonel W. P. Drury, of the Royal Marines, in his book concerning Private Pagett, tells of a large stranded vessel, man-of-war from England, wrecked many years before but still tenanted by a few ancient mariners commanded by an aged midshipman, the only surviving officer. There are just two thoughts in the minds of the sailors. They can never abandon the ship, and they must fire guns at intervals to scare away wild beasts. These cannon are the famous "Guns of Gunapore," the Barisal guns, according to Drury.

Actually the Drury tale was founded on fact. When Captain John Wallis, on his way round the world, touched at Batavia with the *Dolphin* in December, 1767, he found there another King's ship, H.M.S. *Falmouth,* "lying on the mud in rotten condition." She had been there nearly ten years.

Captain Wallis states that the ship was in so decayed a state that she could hardly be expected to survive the next monsoon—only the mud kept her from sinking at her anchors —and her ship's company consisted of no more than a few men, old and broken. Not a single executive officer remained, and of the rest the gunner had died, the boatswain was insane, and the carpenter was dying. The surviving sailors begged Captain Wallis to let them embark with him for home, offering to forfeit the ten years' pay due them, "and go home sweepers, rather than continue the miseries of their present situation." Wallis refused, his excuse being that the *Falmouth* carried government stores on their charge, and they must await orders from England as to the disposal of these before they could quit Batavia. Unfortunately, they had never had an order of any kind from England since their arrival ten years earlier. Wallis sailed away, and nothing more is known of the survivors of the *Falmouth*.

Russell Stone, a summer resident of Saquish, Massachusetts, recalls that several years ago he heard for the first time booming noises coming from a distance. They had no connection, in his opinion, with planes breaking the sound barrier. He has heard the noises ever since during the months of August and September. A Marine veteran, Mr. Stone says that more than anything else the sounds reminded him of distant bombing he had often heard in the South Pacific theatre of war.

It does not seem likely that the Barisal Guns are the result of actual gunfire, or that human agency of any kind is involved. They are probably a natural phenomenon, but whether this condition is in the air, the land, or the sea remains at present an open question. Writing on the subject in 1929, the late Commander R. T. Gould stated: "These sounds may have been produced by aircraft from another planet breaking our sound barrier. Who knows whether the inhabitants of other planets, if there be such, are not far in advance of us scientifically?"

CHAPTER 8

The Maelstrom

The Maelstrom, a very dangerous whirlpool on the coast of
Norway, is on the 68th degree of latitude, in the province
of Nordland and the district of Lofoden, near the island of
Moskoe, from which it also takes the name Moskoe-Ström. Its
violence and roarings can be heard at a great distance and
without any intermission except every sixth hour, at the turn
of high and low water, when it seems to be at a standstill.
During this short interval the fishermen can venture in.
The terrible twisting of the waters soon returns, however,
and no matter how calm the sea may be, the whirlpool gradually increases with such a draft and vortex as to engulf whatever comes within its sphere of action. Ships and men may
be caught in the whirlpool and kept underwater for some
hours. Fragments of the ship, splintered by rocks, then appear, but bodies are rarely seen again.

Many residents of the area imagine that there is an abyss
penetrating the globe, which a writer called Kircher named

the Gulf of Bothnia. But after the most exacting research of the area possible to carry out, it was decided that an abyss going deep into the globe is not possible. This and three other vortices among the Faeroe Islands have no other cause than the collision of waves rising and falling at the flux and reflux against a ridge of rocks and shelves which confine the water so that it precipitates itself like a cataract; and thus the higher the flood rises the deeper the fall must be. The natural result of this is a whirlpool, or vortex, with a terrible suction.

But what has been pulled under remains no longer at the bottom than the ebb lasts. The suction then ceases, and the rising flood tide removes all traces of it and permits whatever had been sunk to make its gradual appearance again.

The following is an account of the Maelstrom written more than a century ago by M. Jonas Ramus:

The mountain of Helseggen, in Lofoden, lies a league from the stream called Moskoe-strőm, from the island Moskoe, which is in the middle of it, together with several nearby isles, as Ambaaren, half a quarter of a league northward, Iflesen, Hocholm, Kieldholm, Suarven, and Buckholm.

Betwixt Lofoden and Moskoe the depth of the water is between thirty-six and forty fathoms; but on the other side, toward Ver, the depth decreases, so as not to afford a convenient passage for a vessel without the risk of splitting on the rocks, which happens even in the calmest weather; when it is flood the stream runs up the country between Lofoden and Moskoe with a boisterous rapidity; but the roar of its impetuous ebb to the sea is scarce equalled by the loudest and most dreadful cataracts; the noise being heard several leagues off, and the vortices or pits are of such an extent and depth that if a ship comes within its attraction it is inevitably absorbed and carried down to the bottom, and there beat to pieces against the rocks; and when the water relaxes, the fragments thereof are thrown up again.

But these intervals of tranquility are only at the turn of the ebb and flood, and calm weather; and last but a quarter of an hour, its violence gradually returning. When the stream is most boisterous, and its fury heightened by a storm, it is dangerous to come within a mile of it. Boats, ships, and yachts have been carried away.

It likewise happens frequently that whales come too near the stream and are overpowered by its violence; and then it is impossible to describe their howlings and bellowings in their fruitless struggles to disengage themselves. A bear once attempting to swim from Lofoden to Moskoe, with a design of preying upon the sheep at pasture in the island, afforded the life spectacle to the people; the stream caught him and bore him down, whilst he roared terribly, so as to be heard on shore.

Large stocks of firs and pine trees, after being absorbed by the current, rise again, broken and torn to such a degree as if bristles grew on them. This plainly shows the bottom to consist of craggy rocks, among which they are whirled to and fro. In the year 1645, early in the morning of Sexagesima Sunday, it raged with such noise and impetuosity that on the island of Moskoe the very stones of the houses fell to the ground.

An unidentified American captain gives the following description:

I had occasion some years since to navigate a ship from the North Cape to Drontheim, nearly all the way between the islands or rocks and the main. On inquiring of my Norwegian pilot about the practicability of running near the whirlpool, he told me that with a good breeze it could be approached near enough for examination without danger, and I at once determined to satisfy myself.

I had been seated but a few moments, when my ship entered the dish of the whirlpool. The velocity of the water altered her course three points toward the center, although she was going three knots through the water. This alarmed me extremely for a moment. I thought destruction was inevitable. She, however, answered her helm sweetly, and we ran along the edge, the waters foaming round us in every form, while she was dancing gaily over them.

The sensations I experienced are difficult to describe. Imagine to yourselves an immense circle running round, of a diameter of one and a half miles, the velocity increasing as it approximates toward the center, and gradually changing its dark blue color to white—foaming, tumbling, rushing to its vortex, very much concave, as much so as the water in a tunnel when half run out; the noise, too, hissing, roaring, dashing all pressing on the mind at once, presented the most awful, grand, and solemn sight I ever experienced. We were near it about eighteen minutes, and in sight of it two hours. It is evidently a subterranean passage. From its magnitude, I should not doubt that instant destruction would be the fate of a dozen of our largest ships, were they drawn in at the same moment. The pilot says that several vessels have been sucked down.

One resident of Norway, Peter Arneson, almost lost his life when caught on the very edge of the Maelstrom in the year 1834. Because of his experience, he later claimed, his hair went from jet black to snow white in six hours.

Aboard a schooner-rigged smack of seventy tons, he and his two brothers, Fredrik and Niels, found fishing in the general vicinity of the Moskoe-strőm extremely lucrative, but, of course, they had to be very careful not to be caught in the terrible vortex. Aboard the fishing smack they often caught more in a single day than others could in an entire week.

On July 20, 1834, the three men started out from their anchorage early that morning in a gentle breeze, which blew from the southwest. A good load of fish was soon aboard. Suddenly, when the men were starting for home just a short time after two o'clock, a fresh wind hit their starboard quarter and soon increased to hurricane strength. They could do nothing against it. Then a strange sight was seen in the heavens, a copper-colored cloud.

The cloud came at them with terrible velocity, and in less than a minute a new storm hit them. It was soon so dark that they could not see each other a few feet away. Both masts went by the board, and when the mainmast broke off, the youngest brother, Niels, was lost in the sea. The boat had a flush deck, with a small hatch in the bow, but the hatch had been battened down, and that saved the two survivors.

The gale swept them into that terrible area where the Maelstrom is located. Peter's older brother, Fredrik, was the first to realize what was happening.

"Moskoe-strőm, moskoe-strőm!" he shrieked, and Peter heard him even above the roar of the storm. Peter said later that he began to shake from head to foot as he realized they were heading right for the terrifying vortex. Desperately figuring their chances, Peter estimated that they would be driven by the gale to the whirlpool at the time of its slack, and there was a possible chance of survival. Suddenly, in the sky, the heavens brightened, and a full moon burst out from behind a retreating cloud. It was a terrible scene which the moon lighted up, and Peter glanced at his watch, which said seven o'clock.

Then brother Fredrik shouted, "Listen!" and Peter heard the roaring whirl of the Maelstrom. His watch had run down, it was behind the time of slack, and they were doomed, for the Maelstrom was in full fury!

Now about a fifth of a mile dead ahead, the Maelstrom was far greater in intensity than on an average day. The hurricane had whipped up the vortex into unbelievable turmoil, and the whirlpool no more resembled its usual awesomeness than it did a millpond.

The roaring noise of the water was drowned out by a strange shrill shriek, and Peter knew that they were on the very edge of the surf which is the outer fringe of the Maelstrom. Peter thought that another moment would carry them down into the depths, but for some reason the craft stayed on the extreme edge minute after minute. The boat did not sink into the water at all, but seemed to skim in the manner of a stone skipping across the surface. Her starboard or right side was next to the whirl itself.

Feeling that he was doomed to perish in the whirlpool, a strange calmness came over Peter, and he began to think that in the presence of such a spectacle he had no right to consider his own life. He actually thought of the exploration of the Maelstrom itself, and the idea struck him that he and his brother would find out its secret, although perishing in the attempt.

Around and around the fringe of the whirlpool the schooner went, until more than a full hour had elapsed. In the stern Fredrik clung to a small empty water cask. He now left the cask, went forward, and attached his hands to an iron ring embedded in the deck.

Suddenly the schooner gave a lurch, and rushed headlong down over the edge, entering the Maelstrom itself. Peter uttered a short prayer, and then opened his eyes. Moments later the strange feeling of falling through a void passed, and Peter looked out on a scene of wonderful but terrible beauty.

Balanced halfway down the sloping side of the vortex, the schooner seemed to be kept by the terrifying speed of the whirlpool from going lower. Round and round the vessel went, and every so often the rays of the full moon hit the tiny craft, balanced precariously on the towering walls of the Maelstrom.

As the mad journey continued, Peter noticed that the smack was now on an even keel. Nevertheless, because of the forty-five-degree angle of the whirlpool itself, the craft appeared to be on her beam ends. He glanced every so often toward the bottom of the deep gulf, but the heavy mist or spray prevented him from seeing far down. In spite of the night time, there was a magnificent rainbow. Peter decided that the mist was the result of the mighty sides of the whirlpool coming together, smashing and churning as they collided.

Gradually Peter came to notice other objects on the side of the whirlpool; timbers, trees, shattered remains of ships, boxes, crates, barrels, chairs, and tables. As he watched, it seemed to him that he was not a participant in what was going on, but merely a witness. One by one the objects were sucked down into the lower part of the funnel and disappeared. Suddenly the great wreck of a Dutch merchant ship, which had been at a lower level, was caught in the suction and went down.

Peter began to develop an idea. He recalled the material he had seen thrown up on the shore at Lofoden, having been pulled down and then thrown back by the Moskoe-strőm. Most of the objects had been shattered in unusual ways, but some were not disfigured at all. Peter wondered if some did not reach the bottom before the turn of the tide, could it be possible that they might reach the level of the ocean again in undamaged condition?

He noticed that barrels or cylinder-shaped objects offered much more resistance than those which were larger and flatter. He decided he might have a chance to survive if he lashed himself to the water cask, cut it free, and jumped overboard. He attracted his brother's attention by signs, pointing to the floating barrels that came near, suggesting that it was the only way to save himself. Fredrik refused. Resigning his brother to his fate, Peter leaped with the barrel into the Maelstrom.

About an hour afterward, while Peter had stayed with the barrel, the schooner had gone down and down. Finally it was far below. Then, as Peter watched with overwhelming emotion, the craft sank headlong into the spray and vanished. Some time later the Maelstrom began to flatten out. As the funnel became less and less steep, the whirlpool seemed to slow up in speed and became less violent. By degrees the froth and the rainbow disappeared, the bottom of the gulf slowly rose, and the wind went down. Peter noticed that the moon was about to set in full view of the shores of Lofoden, above the spot where the pool of the Moskoe-strőm had been.

It was the hour of slack—but the sea still heaved in mountainous waves from the effects of the hurricane.

Peter and the barrel were eventually blown across Ström Channel into the fishing grounds, where he sighted a vessel. Drawing near, Peter was discovered by the fishermen, who rescued him. For a long time Peter was speechless from the memory of the horror through which he had just passed. Although he knew the fishermen as his daily companions, his ordeal had changed him so much that they did not recognize him. Raven black the day before, his hair now was as white as snow, and his entire countenance had aged twenty years!

The story told above was used by Boston-born Edgar Allan Poe in his masterful short story, *A Descent into the Maelstrom,* the material for which he is said to have obtained during his interview with a Norwegian seaman on the wharves of Baltimore. Whether or not that seaman was the original Peter Arneson, the sole survivor of that terrible experience, we shall never know.

CHAPTER 9

The Nelson Hoard

In the state of Maine there are several locations where pirates often went ashore, and in at least three of the known areas it is believed substantial hoards of treasure were buried. Gold, silver, and precious stones are probably still secreted in caches, the keys to which are on maps and charts whose puzzles are still unsolved.

Three years ago my wife, Anna-Myrle, our daughter, Dorothy, and I made a delightful overnight stop at the pleasantly situated cottage of our cousin, Mrs. Norman O. Whitehill, on the banks of the Saint Georges River a few miles from Rockland, Maine. The story I finally gathered as a result of that visit forms the background for this chapter.

I discovered that many years ago, on the Cushing side of the Saint Georges River, settlers are said to have found what they considered was an artificial underground cave with a subterranean passageway right down to the water's edge. My informant told me that some years ago an author, Aubigne

The author with a model of a Spanish galleon, similar to that which still lies hidden in the Florida Everglades. (*Ch. 1*)

Captain Jenkins, whose story that a Spanish captain had torn off his ear was used by the British as propaganda to promote war against Spain in 1739. (*Ch. 2*)

Comte Jean François de Galaup de la Pérouse, commissioned by the French King Louis XVI to lead the ill-fated expedition of the *Boussole* and *Astrolabe*. (*Ch. 3*)

An artist's rendition of how the *Boussole*, La Pérouse's flagship, may have met her end after disappearing from Botany Bay in 1788. (*Ch. 3*)

An artist's reconstruction of the wreck of the *Astrolabe,* which disappeared in the Pacific. (*Ch. 3*)

Coins believed to have been recovered from the wreck of one of La Pérouse's vessels. (*Ch. 3*)

The wreck of pirate Captain Edward Nelson's vessel on the shores of Prince Edward Island, where he is believed to have buried rich treasure which has never been found. (*Ch. 9*)

Mary Ann Arnold who renounced her petticoats to serve as a cabin "boy" on the Sunderland collier *Williams*. (*Ch. 11*)

Jeanette, who fought as a man beside her husband at the Battle of Trafalgar, until her grief at his death betrayed her sex. (*Ch. 11*)

Miss Lucy Brewer who served aboard the *Constitution* (right) during the War of 1812 without it ever being discovered that she was a woman. (*Ch. 11*)

The ship-of-the-line *Bombay* which was destroyed by a mysterious fire at sea. (*Ch. 12*)

It was in a bleak Antarctic terrain such as this that Captain Last found the icebound wreck of the *Starry Crown* with her wealth of gold. (*Ch. 13*)

The U.S.S. *Mount Hood* (AE-11) blows up with 4,500 tons of explosives at 0803, 10 November 1944 in Seeadler Harbor, Manus, Admiralty Islands. (*Ch. 19*)

A wounded man is lowered into an LCVP from the U.S.S. *Mindanao* after she was riddled by flying fragments from the mysterious explosion of the *Mount Hood*. (*Ch. 19*)

Dreaded Sable Island, the Atlantic's graveyard of ships, photographed from the air by Edward Rowe Snow. (*Ch. 23*)

A 400 pound cannon brought to Sable Island by the convicts who came with the Marquis de la Roche to fight bitter battles between themselves. (*Ch. 23*)

Sketch of a wreckers' den on Sable Island. (*Ch. 23*)

The submarine *O-9* which sank during a test dive off the coast of Maine on June 20, 1941, carrying thirty-three men to their deaths. (*Ch. 24*)

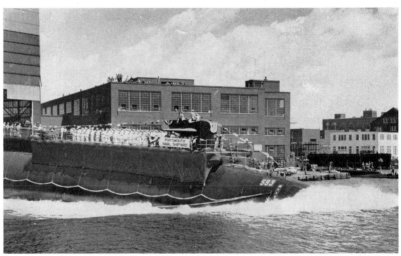

The launching of the ill-fated submarine *Thresher* at Portsmouth Naval Shipyard. (*Ch. 24*)

The nuclear submarine *Thresher* (SSN593) at sea. She was lost during a test dive off the New England coast on April 10, 1963, with 129 persons aboard. (*Ch. 24*)

The U.S.S. *Preserver* tows the bathyscaph *Trieste* from Boston to dive in search of the *Thresher* in the area where she was lost, latitude 41 degrees, 45 minutes North, longitude 65 degrees West. (*Ch. 24*)

Lermond Packard, who made an intensive study of the entire area, was convinced that pirates did bury treasure somewhere along the banks of the river, probably at or near the cave.

On the other hand, a long talk which I had on April 1, 1963, with Clarence Dyer of Tenants Harbor gave me the opinion that few present residents of the area believe that treasure is buried in the region of the cave.

Wholly different from anything that the Indians might have constructed, the cave was assumed by many to have been dug out by pirates. Later called the Pirate's Cellar, the cave was probably the headquarters where the pirates met and divided their spoils. Some local historians always thought that treasure was secreted inside the cave. Nothing was ever found of value in the cave, however, and scores of treasure hunters have dug in the general vicinity unsuccessfully.

The only pirate ever actually known to have been in the area was Captain Edward Nelson, a native of Charlottetown, Prince Edward Island. Nelson was the son of a well-to-do Islander. Every fall after the year 1819, when the lad was seven, the boy's father sent Edward down to Halifax aboard a ship with a load of fruit and produce for the market there.

Unfortunately, the elder Nelson did not realize just what social activities were possible at Halifax during the week the schooner was being unloaded. When Edward was nineteen, Mr. Nelson made his son captain of the schooner, not an unusual promotion in those days. However, Edward's interest in gay night life at Halifax, where he was away from parental restrictions, became greater with his assumption of complete authority on the schooner, now the scene of lively parties and dances.

Edward married a local girl in Charlottetown, and by her had two daughters. They built a house not far from his father's residence, and Edward was given a substantial section of the Nelson estate at the time.

Meanwhile, the annual fruit and produce evening parties at Halifax soon became the talk of the city. News of these eventually reached Prince Edward Island, with the dancing and drinking sprees reported in great detail to the patriarch of the family. When he found out that Edward was spending considerable time in the company of young ladies of questional reputation, Mr. Nelson was shocked. He was particularly grieved by the wording of one document which has been preserved. It stated that Edward was "very wild and drank and intrigued with the girls in an extravagant manner."

The day of reckoning came, a family quarrel resulted, and Edward and his father parted company. It was discovered that Edward had squandered a good portion of the receipts of the last voyage, and because of this the farewells were particularly bitter. He never saw his mother or father again.

Through the assistance of one of his male associates at the evening parties, Nelson obtained a position as lieutenant in the Nova Scotia Fencibles at Halifax. Moving there, he left his wife and children in Charlottetown to live on the rents they collected from the property Edward now owned.

At Halifax he met a Scotsman named Ansel Morrison in whose company he was often seen. Then both men suddenly vanished, and Halifax saw them no more.

The two men had become pirates!

Capturing a trim "little New York battleship" which carried ten guns, they quickly got together a crew of fifty ruf-

fians and joined the brotherhood of pirates "on the account."
They began by treating their captives well but soon had a
reputation for showing them little mercy.

Their first important capture was a trim brig belonging
to a Mr. Hill of Rotherhithe, England. Putting aboard a
prize crew, they sailed the vessel down to New York where
they sold both her and the cargo for a tidy profit.

A cruise to the West Indies followed. Here, in the space of
two years, seventeen ships from Holland and England were
captured. By this time Nelson and Morrison had become de-
praved savages. Their methods of torturing the sailors and
passengers were diabolical, but they would usually save the
lives of the prettiest ladies aboard for their own purposes.
As the months went by and new women were captured, they
would dispose of the ladies taken from former ships by the
simple expedient of throwing them overboard.

One day they landed on the island of Saint Kitts, where
they plundered and set afire two Dutch plantations, murder-
ing the men and slaves. From this island they took more
than thirty women.

Voyaging back toward Nova Scotia, they captured no less
than ten more vessels, all of which they sailed into New York
where the ships were sold for handsome profits. On several
occasions the pirates would sail to the Saint Georges River,
where they would go ashore at several locations and relax,
far from the cares of piracy.

After more successful voyages Nelson's personal fortune
reached the equivalent of $760,000. Morrison was not far
behind, having amassed $580,000.

By this time, both men were actually tiring of their life
of looting and carousing, and while off the coast of Brazil

they suddenly agreed to end their partnership and leave the sea forever. It was arranged that each should go his separate way. Morrison stated that he wished to return to Aberdeen, Scotland, which he had left twenty years before, while Nelson now admitted that he was anxious to resume his relationship with his wife and children, whom he had not seen for many years.

A discussion was held on board the pirate vessel concerning the plan of action for Edward. It was decided that the pirates would sail to the Saint Georges River where Nelson's treasure would be unloaded and buried. The pirate vessel then would proceed to Charlottetown to put Nelson ashore, after which Morrison and the other pirates would sail across to Scotland.

As they approached New York, however, Nelson decided to go ashore. He made arrangements to purchase a country estate, whose owners had perished in a shipwreck. Soon he rejoined his companions aboard the ship, and they sailed for Maine. Reaching Portland, they paid off the entire crew with the exception of fourteen men who were needed to handle the vessel.

Then they sailed back to the Saint Georges River and unloaded the bulk of Nelson's fortune. Six men put the treasure in the long boat, and after carrying it ashore they dug a great hole and buried the loot, Nelson carefully identifying the location on a map he drew in the lower left corner of a chart. The sound of six shots was heard by those aboard the pirate craft, and when Nelson returned to the beach he was alone.

"The others tried to run away," Nelson stated unabashed,

and the sailors realized that he had wished no living witnesses to the burial of his treasure.

Always a careful man, Nelson had kept out about $70,000 of his loot, and it was still aboard when the remnants of the pirate band sailed away from the Saint Georges River forever.

A week later they were approaching Prince Edward Island. A storm came up that night which increased in violence before morning, and the ten men were unable to control their vessel. Soon the craft was wallowing in the trough of the seas, and the men abandoned all hope of escaping.

Crashing ashore on a small island some distance from Charlottetown, the ship went to pieces. Although seven of the pirates drowned, including Morrison, Nelson and two others escaped. Morrison's treasure went down with the ship, but Nelson managed to retrieve his remaining wealth. Unfortunately, the chart with his map on it had been reduced to a mass of pulp by the salt water and was worthless.

Making his way overland with his two assistants, Nelson decided it would be wise to pay them $5,000 each and get them off the island before revealing himself to his wife and family. The three men hired a rig and made their way to Charlottetown, where they stayed at an inn.

Soon the weekly boat to the mainland took the two pirates away. Nelson then left the inn and hired a team to take him home. He was warmly received by his incredulous wife, who introduced him to his two daughters. She then told him that both his father and mother had passed away.

After explaining to his wife and other living relatives that he was now a successful merchant captain, he told his family that he had plans to move to Boston, Massachusetts. The happy woman agreed, and Nelson sold his entire estate. The family then left Prince Edward Island.

Eventually landing in Boston, the Nelsons went up into the town, and took rooms at an inn. After the ship which had brought them sailed away for Halifax, Nelson made arrangements to take his family overland by stage to Providence. There they stopped at another inn, and then two days later sailed from Providence to New York.

Nelson now believed he had covered his trail sufficiently. He bought outright the country estate in New York for which he had negotiated, and sent his two daughters to a finishing school. Within three years he was socially prominent and had joined the church.

Later in his life, if we are to believe the records of a contemporary chronicler, Nelson would take a stagecoach every so often to Portland, Maine, after which he would engage a driver and team, and spend his time visiting many of the long fingers of land that included the area which he thought held his treasure. He never solved the mystery as to where he had buried it, possibly because of a great hurricane which had devastated the region a few months after the fortune was placed there. His own activities in legitimate commerce in New York, however, allowed him to maintain himself and his family in a manner they all enjoyed.

Sixty years ago the Saint Georges area was so pock-marked where unsuccessful seekers had dug for the Nelson treasure that it was dangerous to walk after dark in the vicinity for fear of falling into a hole.

The first to dig in the area in the 1880s was Elisha Jackson, a ship sawyer by trade, who had a strange feeling that someday he would find the Nelson hoard. Aubigne Packard, in his delightful book, *The Town That Went to Sea,* tells us that Jackson had a mystical clue which indicated Brown's Point was the place where the treasure had been buried. Once when he thought it was almost within his grasp, he is said to have made an exclamation that broke the spell and ruined his chances of ever finding it.

A point on the eastern side of the river was so closely associated with the piratical tradition that it was given and still bears the name Treasure Point. Members of one expedition after another have dug and dug but found nothing. Nor is the Nelson hoard the only one connected with the Saint Georges River. A local sea captain who came across a treasure chart a sailor was studying on his ship became convinced that it was a chart of the Saint Georges River. On his return home he secured metal rods and hastened to the spot supposedly marked on the map. A trench fifteen or twenty feet long, however, failed to reveal the hidden fortune, which may still be waiting for you!

No one has ever found a single coin of Edward Nelson's substantial hoard, which obviously was buried not far from where his schooner anchored. Perhaps someday someone will solve the mystery and discover this rewarding cache, but I doubt it.

CHAPTER 10

The *Lilloise* and the *Baychimo*

The efforts made early in the nineteenth century by the French to rescue M. de Blosseville and his companions lost in the Arctic aboard the brig-of-war *Lilloise* aroused the admiration of the entire world. In 1833 the *Lilloise* had sailed on a voyage of discovery to the Arctic Ocean and never returned.

During the fishing season the French government annually sent a vessel of war to the coast of Iceland to protect the fishermen and to render assistance to those who should meet with disaster. The officer dispatched on this service was M. de Blosseville, the most promising scientific officer in the entire French navy.

He was instructed by the French government to avail himself of the opportunity to explore a part of the coast of Greenland and to further the cause of science by making observations and collecting objects of natural history. In July, 1833, Blosseville sailed from Dunkirk in the brig-of-war *Lil-*

loise, having on board a crew chosen for efficiency. After reaching Iceland, the *Lilloise* remained a few days among the fishing vessels. Then de Blosseville proceeded westward to the coast of Greenland, where the ship was battered and damaged in a gale of wind. After returning to Vapnafiord in Iceland for repairs, de Blosseville sent a report of his activities to the minister of marine. This report was the last communication received from the *Lilloise.*

The brig was seen after this, however, on the fourteenth of August under double-reefed topsails with her lower sails close-hauled. The last time she was recognized was on August 25.

The *Lilloise* did not return in the autumn. In the spring of 1834, the French government dispatched the brig-of-war *Bordelaise* to search for the missing vessel, with the command of the expedition given to Captain Dutaillis, an experienced officer. His official account of the search as given to Admiral de Rigny, the minister of marine, was translated several years later, and I include excerpts from that report:

As I was almost entirely without previous exact information, which might guide my steps, or throw light on my operations, I have often been obliged to seek for a rule of conduct in the reasonings and suggestions of the moment. The elements which were wanting, I have hoped to supply by zeal and activity; and I have the presumption to believe that the *Bordelaise* has exhausted all the means at her disposal to obtain what was expected of her investigations.

The complete obscurity which envelops the fate of M. de Blosseville very naturally conducts the mind to form the following conjectures:—

First. That the *Lilloise,* anterior to the 4th of August, 1833, after having met with great damages, and forced to harbor a second time in one of the ports north or west of Iceland, had been detained there by the ice, or state of the vessel.

Second. Or, having been arrested by the ice on the coast of Greenland, the crew would have been able, in the most favorable supposition, to gain the land and reach a Danish colony, and return by one of those vessels that carry on the whale fishery in the west.

Third. Or, that she had perished at sea by one of those unfortunate occurrences so frequent in those parts.

The first of these conjectures being already strengthened by the information furnished at Dunkirk, appearing to be founded on the most probable basis, my first endeavors will be directed towards the verification of these indications; and afterwards I shall examine what degree of certainty can be accorded to the two others.

Setting out from Dunkirk on the 7th of May, 1834, I steered first to Vapnafiord, as my instructions prescribed, where I arrived on the 22d. I expected to receive at this place, which was the last officially-known stopping-place of the *Lilloise,* more complete details concerning her; but my expectations were deceived. The rigors of an arctic winter had cut off the inhabitants from all communication with the northern part of the island, and nothing relating to this vessel had arrived at this station after her departure from it. I learnt, a little while after, from a French brig that was lying there at the same time, that the *Lilloise* new planked certain parts of her bows, and strengthened them with iron. Of this there is no question, as, according to the report of M. de Blosseville, received in France, it was an injury to the bowsprit lashings.

Having accomplished my object at Vapnafiord, and being convinced that if the *Lilloise* had put in, it must be in some one of the bays to the north or west, I sailed, on the 26th, to attempt the passage of Cape Lauganas, notwithstanding the warning I had received from the presence of ice upon all this coast. But I flattered myself that the reports which were made to me had been exaggerated, and that by great precaution I should effect my projects. Unluckily, on the 28th, I ascertained to a certainty that the ice in fact extended from the N.E. to the W.S.W. of the compass, and that all access was become impossible.

There remained to me but two alternatives; either to wait until the heavy gales had shattered the mass, or sail round the island immediately, by passing to the south. As the mercury in the barometer indicated a series of fine days, and knowing that it was not uncommon for the navigation of the northern coast to be shut up during a whole year, I adopted the latter course, as affording the best chance of success, and soon had reason to congratulate myself on the resolution I had taken; for, in visiting a great number of French vessels I met on my route, I received some very valuable information from the captains, which all tended to prove to me that the *Lilloise* had been seen after her departure from Vapnafiord, beating about with winds from the W.S.W., on a N.W. tack.

The most important thing that Captain Dutaillis learned was that Captain Deranjo of the fishing corvette *L'Envie* on one occasion was very close to the *Lilloise*. At the time he observed that the *Lilloise* had two reefs in her topsails, and that the lower sails were close-hauled.

On the fourteenth of June Captain Dutaillis got under way and on that day and the following day beat about the bay. Finding five French ships there, he learned from them that there was no communication with the shore in the direction of Cape Nord. He then sailed to Scutuls Fiord, where he was given information that the *Lilloise* had anchored in the Gulf of Brede Bugt some time before August 14.

He learned that Captain Lamestre of the *Bien Aimée* had found at Hope Bugt a piece of chain cable, a copper kettle, and a piece of wood circled with iron. All of this had come ashore in the year 1833.

Another attempt was made to try to discover the *Lilloise* in the summer of 1835. Captain Trehouart of the corvette *Recherche* made a fruitless voyage along the western coast of Iceland, reaching the eastern coast of Greenland. He had left Cherbourg April 17, to arrive off the southern coast of Iceland on May 7, leaving Reykjavik on the eighteenth of May.

Captain Trehouart then heard that a Dutch captain had been told by a sailor of Dunkirk that he had seen "the *Lilloise* perish." Unable to check the report in any way, Trehouart discovered that men on a Dutch fishing vessel on which the sailor later worked were said to have seen the *Lilloise* sink some miles out in the ice. On attempting to check this information he was told by the gizelleman * in the bay that no such information had ever come to him. He was in charge of the entire bay, visiting all vessels which entered, and knew every captain of the Dutch vessels which fished that coast, but he had never heard them speak of the shipwreck of the *Lilloise*.

At the same time Captain Trehouart visited seven Dutch vessels. No one aboard any of the craft knew anything about the *Lilloise*. Therefore Captain Trehouart decided that no Dutch sailor or captain on any Dutch vessel had seen the *Lilloise* sink, and the rumor was incorrect.

* Gizellemen had duties similar to harbor masters in the United States.

He now sent M. Gaimard ashore to explore the various cliffs and bays in the area. Finally, after the latter had reported complete failure, the *Recherche* was steered toward Steneuts Fiord, but the quest ended with no success at all. It now seemed apparent that if the *Lilloise* had perished anywhere around this area, fragments of her wreckage would have come ashore, and the people must have noticed them. This was not the case, as there was no report of wreckage.

Captain Trehouart of the *Recherche* decided that on the twenty-ninth of July, 1833, the *Lilloise* had probably reached latitude 68.30 on the 28th longitude, where open ice was found. On the fourth of August, the *Lilloise* left Vapnafiord, where she had put in to repair the damage to her bowsprit. Probably by August 14 she was near the parallel of Cape Nord. Therefore the *Recherche* was sent out to the NNE, but nothing was found.

The French government, now desperate to find either the *Lilloise,* her crew, or news about her, once more sent out the *Recherche* in the spring of 1836. The French government published the following ordinance:

First. That a reward of one hundred thousand francs shall be bestowed on the French or foreign navigators who may restore the whole or a part of the officers and crew of the *Lilloise.*
Second. That a reward proportioned to the service rendered shall be given to those who may announce the first correct intelligence of them, or who may restore to France any papers or effect, whatever, which have belonged to this expedition.

Captain Trehouart soon encountered a Dutch galiot, *William the First,* and Captain Vankeulen told him that the name of the man who had seen a French brig-of-war capsize August 28, 1833, off Cape Staalbierg was Pierre de Goede and that de Goede had often spoken of this wreck.

The *Recherche* now sailed for the west coast of Greenland. The first ice was met on the thirtieth of June, which soon surrounded the vessel on all sides. In attempting to get out, the *Recherche* crashed into a berg, but made no water, although her hull was damaged. Dispatching an Eskimo fisherman to get a pilot, the captain of the *Recherche* anchored in an excellent roadstead.

M. Moller, in charge of a small settlement in the area, now wrote the following letter for the *Recherche* to take:

M. le Governor: Captain Trehouart has requested me to inform you by letter, the opinion which I entertain of the possibility that the crew of the *Lilloise* may have been able to save themselves; and I have therefore the honor to state to you, that although such an event is not probable, it is not at all impossible that some of the crew of this brig may be so fortunate as to reach the eastern coast of Greenland on the ice; more particularly, if they had light boats, provisions, and clothing to protect them against the cold, during many days' exposure on the ice.

Should any in this manner be so fortunate as to gain the land, it will not be impossible, that, under favorable circumstances, they may have passed along the coast to Frederickshaal; and there is no doubt that in this passage they would find many inhabitants of the eastern coast from whom they would derive assistance to continue their route. In this case, I have had the honor of informing the captain that there is no doubt, if the crew are so fortunate as to reach Julienshaal, they will be treated by the Danish servants in the best manner the circumstances of the place will admit; and that an account of them will be sent to the royal mercantile office of Greenland, at Copenhagen, and thence to the French legation.

Captain Trehouart had to leave Frederickshaal without getting an answer to his quest, and finally he returned to Reykjavik where he stayed until September 3.

All hopes of rescuing the *Lilloise* were now considered gone, and the name of that unfortunate vessel was formally erased from the list of the French navy. Although we will never know what her fate was, the most probable conjecture is that she went down off the coast of Iceland. A report was for some time prevalent that a stone had been found on the coast of Greenland, on which was a rudely carved inscription, purporting to have been done by some of her unfortunate company; but this and many other rumors which reached France, could never be authenticated.

Almost one hundred years separate the *Lilloise* and the *Baychimo*. Both vessels are concerned with the Arctic Ocean. The *Lilloise* disappeared entirely, while the *Baychimo* keeps reappearing.

Mr. John R. Herbert, editor of the *Patriot Ledger,* published in Quincy, Massachusetts, obtained details for me concerning the deserted ghost ship *Baychimo,* a 1,300-ton vessel which still haunts the Arctic wastes.

Belonging to the Hudson Bay Company, this trim, solid, steel cargo steamer left Vancouver, British Columbia, early in July, 1931. The *Baychimo* passed through the Bering Strait, after which she entered the Northwest Passage by way of the

Beaufort Sea. She spent hundreds of thousands of dollars buying furs along the Victoria Land coast. Then when October weather threatened, she began her long return trip back toward Vancouver.

The *Baychimo,* with her long high prow, had a curved bridge, and was considered the finest craft possible for battling the pack ice and floes of the area. A pioneer in fur trading with Eskimo settlements around the Beaufort Sea, she pushed through the mighty ice floes on many occasions as she journeyed back and forth on several of the most treacherous marine routes in the world. Each year she delivered supplies of food, fuel, and clothing in exchange for pelts, visiting regularly eight of the Hudson Bay outposts.

On the sixth of July, 1931, she left Vancouver, British Columbia, with Captain John Cornwall and thirty-six crew members. Reaching the last post of her eastward run, the *Baychimo* then started back for Vancouver.

Unfortunately, the ship found herself caught in an early winter pack-ice formation. Captain Cornwall, her commanding officer, made a survey of the area and discovered a collection of huts on the mainland only 700 yards from the place where the ship was caught in the ice. He moved his crew and enough provisions ashore to last the winter.

On November 26 a terrible blizzard hit the settlement, and for the next two days the swirling snow and below-zero temperatures prevented even the hardiest sailor from venturing out.

Finally, the blizzard ended. When the first man went down to the beach, he found to his amazement that the *Baychimo* was free of ice. The crew went aboard, and for several hours the sailors headed her west. Then the pack ice began to build up again, and the crew was marooned again. On October 8 the great frozen area developed a fault line. The *Baychimo* moved toward shore, and it appeared to be only a matter of time before the vessel would be crushed.

On October 15 the Hudson Bay Company sent two aircraft from Nome, 588 miles away, and twenty-two of the crew were flown back to Nome. Captain Cornwall, her skipper, and fourteen men were left behind to stay with the ship.

The master of the *Baychimo* and his crew now built a small shelter on the pack ice. On November 24 another terrible blizzard hit the area, and when the storm went down, the men discovered to their dismay that their ship had completely vanished.

Abandoning their hut, they started for the mainland. They encountered an Eskimo, who told them that he had seen their ship some forty-five miles away to the west. They hiked with the Eskimo to the location he had given, and surely enough, there was the *Baychimo*. Captain Cornwall took as many choice furs off her as he could and then flew home with his crew.

The next we hear of the *Baychimo* is when Leslie Melvin discovered her in 1932. On March 12 of that year this young trapper and explorer found her on a journey he was making from Herschel Island to Nome by dog team. Boarding her, Melvin found that much of her fur cargo was still intact in her hold. As Melvin was alone, he left the *Baychimo* and continued his journey.

The next contact with the *Baychimo* was made some time later by a group of wandering prospectors who sighted her and went on board. Then in March, 1933, twenty-eight Eskimos found that the ship had drifted back to where Captain

Cornwall had abandoned her. Another whirling blizzard hit the vessel, marooning for ten days the Eskimos aboard her. Finally the storm went down, and the Eskimos got away.

Miss Isobel Hutchinson, a Scottish botanist, sighted the *Baychimo* from a schooner in July, 1934, went aboard the craft, and remained for several hours. Little is known of what she found at the time.

By September, 1935, the steamer was off the Alaskan coast. More than four years later, in November, 1939, Captain Hugh Polson spotted her from a distance. He was able to board her successfully but as a storm was approaching he was unable to salvage her, and when the storm subsided, the *Baychimo* had vanished.

It is said that the *Baychimo* has been seen more than fifty-six times in the last sixteen years. Each time she has eluded whatever pursuit was possible, and seems destined to continue her evasive action. Over the past thirty-one years she has sailed, crewless and alone, many thousands of miles in the Far North.

On March 11, 1962, fishermen found the *Baychimo* in the Beaufort Sea. They left her to drift away into the unknown, and for the past year she has been unreported.

CHAPTER 11

Girls Disguised as Men

In his delightful volume, *Thar She Blows,* the New Bedford author Chester Howland has a strange story of a girl who served aboard a whaler as a man until under dramatic circumstances it was found out she was a woman. Actually, although not generally known, this deception was practiced at sea far more often than is usually believed.

The unsolved mystery, of course, is how did the girls get away with their disguise? In the intimate quarters before the mast it seems utterly nonsensical to assume that a girl could pretend she was a man week after week, month after month, and in some cases year after year.

Four instances of this type of deception, are narrated in this chapter, beginning with Chester Howland's lady whaler. Then comes the French female Jeanette, after which you may read of a girl who served on the *Robert Small.* The fourth young lady was on the frigate *Constitution* for a three-year period.

One day in the New Bedford Public Library author Howland was reading the pages of the New Bedford Standard of the Civil War period. Turning the pages, he came across an unusual drawing. It was of the actual discovery by the officers of the whaling bark *America* that a member of the crew believed to be a man was in reality a woman! Chester Howland stresses the Victorian nature of the drawing, which shows a fully clothed girl tied to the mast in preparation for a flogging.

Not only would the picture fail to catch a reader's eye today, but it was not accurate in any way. Although the lady in the sketch is apparently terribly embarrassed at the discovery and the officers and men are standing with mouths agape, a flogging aboard a whaler was not executed as is indicated in the sketch. For a group of seamen ordered to get ready to administer a flogging, it was a rough activity. First, the person to be flogged was spread-eagled against the ship's mast. Then all clothes down to the waist were ripped off, and the cat-o'-nine-tails was made ready for the announced number of lashes on the recipient's bare back.

When this was done aboard the *America,* of course, the female contours of the lady in question were definitely revealed in an unmistakable manner, and the flogging was stopped then and there.

The story begins when recruits were needed on the whaling bark *America,* announced as preparing to sail on a three-year cruise in search of the world's largest mammal. Her master, Captain Luce, was soon to set out from Edgartown, and because of the Civil War then raging, it was becoming difficult to assemble a full ship's company.

George Weldon signed on, but George in reality was an

eighteen-year-old girl. Whether or not her real name was Weldon was never known, but by the time the *America* was at sea, Miss Weldon was carrying out her duties successfully. With her closely cropped hair and special undergarments which flattened her breasts, she attracted no suspicious glances, or so the story goes. Her voice was low-pitched, which added to the illusion. Thus we see that Miss George was a run-of-the-mill sailor who attracted no attention one way or another. She took her turn in all shipboard duties, and could usually do her share in the whaleboat, pulling as strongly as most of the others.

Deeper and deeper the *America* sailed into the South Atlantic, and when the whaler reached latitude 46° south, the incident occurred which ended Miss George's career as a sailor on the *America*.

She had been rowing with the others in chase of a whale, but the whaleboat was having trouble getting within harpooning distance. At two o'clock that particular afternoon of January 9, 1863, another whale broke water a hundred yards away, and the mate shouted for the oarsmen to close the distance.

Suddenly Miss George could row no more and relaxed her hold on the oar. The mate shouted at her, and there was a scuffle. Author Howland tells us how she swung her great oar so that it struck the officer a smashing blow. He sprawled headlong overboard into the sea, but was hauled into the boat at once.

When the whaleboat returned, all hands were called on deck by the captain.

"Weldon," he said in a hard voice, "striking an officer is

mutiny aboard this or any other ship. You are to be punished."

There was grumbling among some members of the crew, but the captain paid no attention to it. Addressing the chief mate, he continued: "Mr. Cottle, trice him thumbs up to the rigging. Now, bare his back for a dozen lashes. Lay them on heavy! We propose to have order on this craft."

George was handled roughly and a surge of blood showed crimson on her face when Mr. Cottle spread-eagled her to the mizzen shrouds. When the men ripped her shirt off, they stopped suddenly, for her true identity was revealed. Her face went pale, and she sagged, unconscious, held upright in the rigging by the cords about her thumbs. Of course, the rope's end never reached its target, and the girl was cut down at once!

Later that day Captain Luce made the following entry in the log book:

Bark *America* in the South. Friday, January 9, 1863. Commences with light breeze from the west. The boats in chase of whales. At three P.M. the boats came aboard. This day found George Weldon to be a woman, the first I ever suspected of such a thing. Later part breezes from the south by west. Took in sail. Steering east-southeast. Three sail in sight.

At the battle of Trafalgar a French ship caught fire, and the crew made every effort to escape from the flames. British frigates and schooners sent their boats to save as many lives as possible. Among those who were thus preserved from a watery grave was a young French woman who was brought on board a British man-of-war in a state of complete nakedness.

Although it was in the midst of battle, she received every assistance possible. Nothing, however, could be done to clothe her until the battle ended and the officers got to their sea chests. She was soon given sheets and supplied with needles and thread to fashion clothing for herself. Curtains from the officers' cots were made into gowns and other garments. By degrees she was made as comfortable as circumstances would admit, and was later asked to tell her story. The following is the translated statement of the woman who was known as Jeanette:

The combined fleets had received orders to proceed from Cadiz, where they lay, to make an attack upon and capture the British fleet; for from their superior force they were confident of success, and elated at the same time with the idea that it would be but an easy task. That no impediment might be in the way, all the females were ordered to go on shore; I was married and could not endure the thought of quitting my husband. I was resolved, therefore, to share his glory or his death. No time was lost in carrying my plan into execution. Having rigged myself out in a suit of sailor's clothes, thus disguised I entered on board in the same ship with him as a seaman.

In this state I remained, doing duty, during the engagement, when, whilst fighting by the side of my husband, a ball killed him on the spot. On seeing him fall dead, my grief was too much; nature displayed itself, and through excess of emotion I betrayed my sex.

To add to the distresses which the discovery occasioned, an alarm was now spread that the ship was on fire; I cared very little about it, life to me was not desirable. All hands were employed in the endeavour to check the progress of the flames. This seemed to be impossible, and it became necessary to think of the means of escape, for the fire raged with great fury, and there was every probability that, in a few minutes, the ship would be blown into the air, as the fire was fast approaching the powder magazine.

The resolution to take to the water being now unavoidable, the men commenced to undress themselves; in this dreadful situation I was strongly urged to do the same, to make every effort for self-preservation, and it being my only chance. After some entreaty, persuasion, and remonstrance, I summoned sufficient resolution, and began undressing in front of the men, for I either had to do this or perish in the flames.

I was then lowered into the ocean by a rope from the taffrail, the lead of which was melting at the time. Whilst letting me down, some of the lead dropped and burned the back of my neck. On reaching the water, one of my shipmates, a good swimmer, remained by my side. In this manner I was supported until picked up by a boat belonging to a British schooner.

Jeanette came from French Flanders. She remained aboard until the schooner's arrival at Gibraltar, when a cartel ship took her to a Spanish port. Her last name was never revealed. On leaving the ship, her heart seemed overwhelmed with gratitude; she shed an abundance of tears, and could only now and then, with a deep sigh, exclaim "Les bons Anglais."

In the year 1839 a revealing letter was written by an officer of the *Robert Small,* an East Indiaman then off the Cape of Good Hope. The essential part of the letter, dated October 20, follows:

A very singular case has been discovered on board our ship. We have detected a young lady in the person of a sailor who has done duty with our crew from the time we left the Thames until it was found that she belonged to the fair sex.

Her name is Mary Ann Arnold. She is the daughter of the late Lieutenant Arnold, of the Royal Navy, who served in that capacity on board the *Ganges* and *Prince Regent* men-of-war. Being a man of dissolute habits, he lost his commission in consequence, after which he resided with his wife at Sheerness, where, by continuing his habits of dissipation, he and his family were reduced to great distress.

By the intercession of some friends, Mr. Arnold was admitted a pensioner in Greenwich Hospital, in which asylum he died recently. During the latter interval, and after her husband's death, Mrs. Arnold lived at Sheerness, supporting herself and her children by manual labour until the summer of 1835, when, after great exertion in the harvest field, she was attacked by bilious fever and died, leaving her children totally unprovided for. Mrs. Arnold's furniture was sold to pay the expenses of her funeral, and some charitable neighbors took the orphans into their house and supported them for a time.

Mary Ann, the subject of the present statement, was ten years old when her mother died. Partly by labouring in the fields, and partly by going on errands, she at first supported herself, and contributed to the sustenance of her little sister, who was only eight months old when her mother died. Mary Ann next obtained permanent employment in a rope-factory at Sheerness, where she earned two shillings and sixpence a week.

Going frequently in boats, and amongst the shipping, she found that boys of her age, who went to sea, earned more money, were better fed, "thought more of," and in every way in a superior condition to her; and upon this Mary Ann determined to renounce the petticoats, and to become a sailor.

Borrowing an old jacket, trowsers, and shirt from a boy of her acquaintance, to whom she said she was going to have a lark in them, she took leave of the rope-factory and the owner of the clothes without the ceremony of a farewell, and succeeded, to her great joy, in getting employment as a cabin boy, in the *Williams,* a Sunderland collier, then lying at Sheerness.

Mary Ann was kindly treated, and she continued to do the miscellaneous hard work of a collier's cabin boy, abow and abaft for two years and two months, to the satisfaction of six captains, who successively commanded the *Williams* during that period. A seventh captain came, and this time man and boy did not like each other, so Mary Ann forever abandoned the coal marine and its blackamoor service, and on the 22nd of October, 1838, she entered as cabin boy at Shields on board the brig *Anne,* bound for London and Quebec. She made several voyages in this vessel. Unfortunately, the *Anne* was wrecked off Blakeney, in the last equinoctial gales; but the captain and crew had the luck to escape, after enduring great hardships. Returning to Shields, Miss Arnold entered again as a cabin boy in the *Choice,* bound for London, with stores for the *Robert Small,* East Indiaman, in which ship she next succeeded in getting an engagement as a sailor boy the day before she sailed from London.

She has well done her work as a strong, active boy, in this ship. I have seen Miss Arnold amongst the first aloft to reef the mizzen top-gallant sail, during a heavy gale, in the Bay of Biscay. When we crossed the equator, she underwent the ceremony of tarring and shaving in its roughest form. On the 20th of September last, some of the crew expressed suspicions to Captain Scott that the boy Arnold was a girl.

The captain upon this ordered the surgeon to examine the youngster. The surgeon did so, and declared that he was a girl. Miss Arnold then gave the foregoing history of herself. The captain, and all the passengers and crew, praised and pitied her. She was at once prevailed upon to abdicate the sailor's jacket and trowsers, and resume the clothes proper to her sex. She now appears a pretty, bashful girl of fifteen years of age. The lady passengers have given her lots of presents. Her hair is already getting long, and I suppose she will soon think of ringlets.

Captain Scott behaves in the kindest manner to her and he has promised that she shall receive her pay just the same as if she were to continue to do a young mariner's duty during the whole passage out and home. Miss Arnold is, though rather bashful, considering the short time she has had to learn ladies' ways, like other heroes and heroines, capable of being drawn out. I frequently see her surrounded by applauding listeners, while she pitches a long yarn about "the dangers of the sea."

Our heroine has two brothers, older than herself; one is boatswain of the *Royal Adelaide,* the other is carpenter on board the *Britannia,* stationed at Portsmouth. The latter, she says, knew that she had turned sailor, and he approved of the metamorphosis when he saw her in the trust and occupation of cabin boy on board the *Williams.*

The fourth story involving women who sailed on the high seas as men is that of Miss Lucy Brewer who was born in Plymouth, Massachusetts, in the year 1793. Later she married a Mr. Richard West of Kingston, and they settled down in a comfortable home in Duxbury. Mr. West died in 1827.

In the year 1839 a lad named Richard Sturtevant was hired to do manual labor around the West mansion. Some months later, after a particularly hard day of work in the sun, he was offered refreshments of cider and cookies. As he was eating them Mrs. West told him that she had a tale of interest to relate to him, as she did not wish to die and have her true story lost forever:

I am going to tell you tonight something I have never told anyone—except my husband. I feel that I may die at any time, and I shall somehow pass my last days in greater happiness knowing that my mystery will be revealed when I am gone.

My parents, grandparents, brothers and sisters have all passed away and there is no one who can possibly take offense when they learn my true story.

I will start at the very beginning. In the year 1809 when I was sixteen years old I fell in love with a young man who left our town suddenly, and I never saw him again. This broke my heart. I fled to Boston, where I remained for three years, living unhappily on West Boston Hill there.

One day I met a young lieutenant from the frigate *Constitution*. He won my heart, but when he, too, disappeared I determined to follow him aboard the ship.

Thinking that I could fool the enlisting officer, I disguised myself as a man and passed the test. Enlisting on the *Constitution*, I thought all was well until I found that my young man had been transferred the day before to another ship. There was nothing I could do, however, and so I kept my identity secret from everyone and sailed with the others.

I recall the first battle I was in, in August 1812, when the British frigate *Guerrière* lost to our craft. The entire war went by, and the *Java*, the *Pictou*, the *Cyane* and the *Levant* fell to our proud ship.

Well, the war ended and I received my honorable discharge from the service. Back to Plymouth County I went, but not before I stopped at a rooming house in Boston to change to a woman's dress. No one, in the entire three years, had detected that I was really a woman."

It was an unusual story, and for years afterward Richard told it to his children and then his grandchildren as they sat before the fire, and they all thought of the courageous woman who had served aboard the frigate "Old Ironsides."

CHAPTER 12

Fire on the *Bombay*

In 1800, after the disastrous fire and explosion of H.M.S. *Queen Charlotte* off the harbor of Leghorn, Italy, which cost the lives of 673 men, the British government spent many years perfecting a system of fire prevention at sea. This arrangement worked so well that British naval craft were soon considered fireproof. Thus, more than sixty years went by before another battleship became the scene of a holocaust.

In the year 1860 the sailing ship-of-the-line *Bombay*, built of teak in 1827, was cut in two, lengthened, and made into a steamer. It was aboard the *Bombay* that another great conflagration at sea took place. To this day the mystery of the real cause of the disaster is unsolved.

The following eyewitness story of the fire aboard the H.M.S. *Bombay*, as written by Admiral Henry J. Carr, gives a picture of the dangers always present at sea on one of the old wooden ships-of-the-line:

114

Though fire was our most deadly enemy at sea, we always felt perfect confidence in getting the better of it, and that, I need not say, is more than half-way towards doing anything in this world. Where men have to save their lives by their own exertions and coolness, a stout heart is everything.

The *Bombay* was the flag-ship of Rear Admiral Charles Elliott, C.B., on the southeast coast of America; but at the time of the disaster he and his staff were on board H.M.S. *Stromboli,* the *Bombay* having been ordered to sea for a week's exercise with the big guns and in other ways.

We left Monte Video, in the river Plate, early one fine mid-summer morning in December 1864—the season in south latitudes being reversed—with 655 people on board.

Target practice was the first part of our business that day. After beating the retreat from general quarters, at about half past three in the afternoon, a division on the lower deck were kept at their guns for shell practice. They were my quarters, and I was on duty with the division. For the purpose of the exercise the shell room and the after magazines were kept open. We were just looking out for the target through the lower deck ports, and I remember so clearly seeing a French merchant ship going close past us, under all sail.

At this moment the fire bell rang, the signal being formed by rapid strokes on the ship's bell. Now, this bell often rang for drill only, and accordingly there were few who suspected that this time the warning was given in grim earnest. But it was soon clear that it was no summons to an ordinary drill, for one of the petty officers, who was leaving the hold, where he had been employed all the afternoon in passing shells to the guns, had seen a flame in a far corner, right under the magazine. He had at once run up and rung the bell, and reported what he had seen.

Our drills were always done against time, so, with every one in the ship on the alert, and a great part of the crew still at the guns, it was a matter of only two or three minutes to have six or eight large hoses pouring water wherever directed.

My brother officer on the lower deck at the time was Stirling, the gunnery lieutenant—he was lost in 1880 with the *Atalanta* * a small sailing frigate which he commanded, and which is supposed to have foundered in the Atlantic with every soul on board.

I superintended the unloading of the guns. They were old eight-inch muzzle loading, smooth bore weapons, and the only way to extract a charge was to scoop it out—a task which, with these guns, was very difficult. But we got the charges out, except in the case of two guns, which were jammed, and in these the powder and shot had to be left—obviously a serious danger in a burning ship.

When I had seen to the guns I went to the pumps aft on the lower deck, and found that there was fire indeed. Smoke was pouring up from below, and was already so dense that it was almost impossible to see. The men who were directing the hoses were constantly relieved, and were taken up sick or suffocated.

The pumps were heaving bravely round, but the over-powering smoke continued to ascend through the hatchway. The deck became so thick with it that in order to enable us to continue working we had to trice up some of the ports. This could not have been more than five minutes after the

---

* I tell the story of what is known of the *Atalanta*'s loss in *Mysteries and Adventures Along the New England Coast*, pp. 272–275.

outbreak was reported—so fierce and swift was the spread of the flames.

Enormous quantities of water were being poured below— literally tons, for, besides the pumps, there were relays of men with buckets, mess kettles, and dishes at work, filling and emptying their vessels on to the fire. Hammocks, too, were un- lashed on deck, and these, with beds and hundreds of blan- kets, were wetted and sent rapidly below to be used in trying to smother the flames. But the fire, in addition to being so far up in the wing of the hold as to be almost out of reach, had got among a lot of junk—pieces of old cable and cordage and brooms—and sent out volumes of dense smoke.

One of the pumps was not drawing properly, so I got hold of the carpenter, Mr. Ross, and went down the engine room hatchway to the orlop deck—the deck below the lower deck and also below the waterline.

The orlop deck was thick with smoke in every direction, and so intensely hot that it was impossible to remain there, and we were driven away. Already the orlop deck, which was immediately above the fire, was flooded several inches deep, and so was the after magazine.

Now, had there been a moment for thinking, when it was clear to every one that a terrible fire was raging and master- ing the ship, there would have come the appalling knowledge that the after magazine and the forward magazine contained forty tons of powder each, and that we were in momentary peril of being blown into the air with the ship; but, happily, we were too busy to think of anything except the work in hand. When I went up to the lower deck again, we found smoke pouring from the "pigeon holes"—spaces in the old wooden ships which opened from below between the timbers on to the lower deck.

One's impressions at such a time are strange and inexplicable. I remember thinking that, even if the worst came to the worst, and the fire really overwhelmed us, we should be quite safe, as the big French ship was so near us; and my own impression was that, bad as things looked, there was more smoke than fire. We went on steadily doing our best between decks, and at the same time a great part of the ship's company was preparing to hoist out the boats—a precaution which was always taken, even for exercise.

The captain (Colin Campbell, whose early death was so sad for all who knew him) and the commander (John Crawford Wilson, who died while Admiral Superintendent of Devonport Dockyard) now came below to see how matters stood, and it was speedily and abundantly clear that the ship was doomed.

The order "out boats" had found everything in readiness, and when, on all hands being ordered on deck, I got to my station, which was on the quarter deck, I found that the boats were being hoisted out. The cutter was out, the barge hooked on and hoisted out on the port side, then the pinnace and first launch on the starboard side, and all the quarter and stern boats were lowered.

The first launch was forty-two feet long, the largest in the ship, and had been "raised upon"—that is, her gunwales had been heightened, so that she could be fitted with a steam engine. The engine, however—and very fortunately, room being precious—was not in her when she was stowed inboard, because other boats had to go inside her.

Besides five boats, which were hanging outside the ship,

there were six others, large and small, stowed inboard, and
these had to be hoisted out. All were got out square and well
except one, the second launch.

The fire had spread so quickly that the smoke now poured
up in the waist of the ship and completely cut off one end
from the other. An immense help to the flames had been
given by the bursting of casks of rum which were stowed in
the hold in the compartments next to that in which the fire
originated. The bilges, where there was an uninterrupted
flow from one end to the other, were flooded with blazing
spirits, so that the ship was now on fire literally from bow to
stern.

The last large boat was just in the air, though seemingly
on fire, when the flames burst on to the quarter deck, where
I then was, and catching an awning over our heads, ran up
the rigging, instantly setting every rope and sail ablaze. The
tarred ropes and the awning burnt over our heads with a rush,
yards went on end, and spars and burning rigging rattled
down. Still we tried to get the second launch over the side,
although it looked red hot with lurid smoke; but its ropes
burnt, and down it came again—White, the second captain of
the maintop, jumping out as it fell.

The very deck on which we stood was now on fire, and a
brother lieutenant—now Admiral Sir John Fullerton, who
commanded Queen Victoria's yachts, and is an equerry to
the King—and myself were the only officers on the quarter
deck, the captain and the commander having gone to the fore
part of the ship.

The men on the quarter deck made a rush for the starboard gangway, where the pinnace was alongside. These men
were mostly marines, bandsmen, artificers, craftsmen, and so

on—"idlers," as they are called, not being bluejackets. The majority were unable to swim, and it was amongst them that nearly all the deaths occurred.

A large and beautiful white ensign was floating from the peak, union down, in the midst of a thick mass of smoke, as a signal of distress; but the smoke itself was the best announcement of our extremity to three vessels which were in sight, as well as to the land—even to Monte Video in the distance. To swimmers there seemed little danger, for we mostly forgot our greatest danger—the magazines under our feet—and I think that all through it never struck me that I was individually in peril.

Large numbers of men were holding to ropes in the water and to the ship's side. The boats had pulled ahead of the ship with their freights, all but two—the steam launch, a big, unwieldy boat, which was near the stern, and the pinnace, which was close on to the beam, heavily laden with men. The sick had been got into the launch, in which also were a number of officers and men whose duty had been on the poop. Happily, none of the sick was seriously ill.

The falling of burning ropes and spars reminded Fullerton and myself that it was time to be off; but there was a graver signal than that, which was the bursting of shells between decks. In those days we always had two rounds per gun of live shell stowed in boxes between the deck beams.

The roaring of the flames and the crashing of the bursting shells made it necessary for every man to fend for himself. The result was that there was much mad jumping into the water. Of those who sprang overboard, many, being non-swimmers, were paralysed by fear and hurled themselves recklessly into the water. It is a melancholy and significant fact that nearly the whole of the hundred lives which were lost in the catastrophe were those of men who had not learnt to swim and could not help themselves when in the water.

By way of showing the incomprehensible workings of the mind at such a crisis as this, I will mention a strange incident. When Fullerton and myself saw that it was time to go, we got up into the hammock netting and stripped ourselves before jumping into the sea to swim to one of the boats, the arrangement being that Fullerton should make for the pinnace and I for the launch.

We got rid of nearly all our clothes, and then the two of us took our watches and chains and other little things we valued, and secured them in the netting, believing, even then, that we should be able to return to the ship and get them! On the anniversary of the disaster Sir John and I regularly exchange letters, and in his last communication he said how well he remembers this curious mutual trivial act at such a time.

Fullerton safely swam after the pinnace, and I got into the main chains and saw Blake, the doctor, jump overboard out of one of the ports under the poop and make for the launch.

I encouraged the men who were hanging on below me by telling them that they were quite safe, and that the launch would come and pick them up. Two midshipmen, named Strange and Hamilton, were with me. Strange, poor fellow, was afterwards navigating lieutenant with Stirling when he was lost with the *Atalanta*. I told Strange to stand by to swim for the launch; and as for Hamilton—who could not swim—I assured him that he was safe enough, and that we would get him into the launch, which in due time we did.

Just then a shell burst behind us on the main deck, and we

all jumped involuntarily into the water. I made for the launch, and saw Mr. Ross, the carpenter, an enormously fat and very famous old gentleman, who helped to haul me over the lofty bows.

Another celebrated person who was in the launch was Giddy, the chief boatswain's mate. He had in his pocket his watch-bill, a little list of the men of the ship's company, which turned out to be the only list by which we could muster the men afterwards. Every other record of the people on board was lost.

With great difficulty we managed to get the launch up to the ship, having only a few oars, and the current being very strong. The *Bombay*'s anchors had been burnt from their fastenings, and so she had anchored herself. We got in, however, and rescued all the men who were still hanging to the ship's side.

I was too busy with this work to look much about me, but was constantly reminded by others less so in the stern of the boat that the mainmast was falling, the magazine about to blow up, guns going off, and shells exploding. Watts, the master, and myself were therefore glad enough to shove off the moment we had lugged the last terrified non-swimmer over the bows.

On clearing the ship I, for the first time, took in the perfect ruin from which we had escaped. The hull was burning from end to end, flames were roaring out of most of the ports, there were the constant explosions of shells, the mizzenmast seemed about to fall one way and the foremast another, all the stays being burnt, and the masts themselves were on fire in many places. The mainmast, a towering mass of spars, two hundred feet high, and weighing altogether some eighty tons, was leaning right over the spot where we had been, and in another minute fell across the side, and would infallibly have smashed our boat and us too! Surely here a Kind Hand had held it back till we had finished our work.

We had plenty to do, for, as we were the only boat astern of the ship, all the men who were floating on bits of spars, gratings, hammocks, etc., came our way with the tide and were picked up.

We found Poe, a little midshipman, swimming bravely about. He is now a rear admiral, commanding in the East Indies. Then there was Ramsden, another midshipman, on a breaker; and Kelly, the first lieutenant, and engineer M'Garahan were adrift on a hatch which had been thrown overboard. Kelly was very sick, having been stifled in the hold of the ship, and simply lay under the thwarts all the evening. He lived to be an admiral and superintendent at Chatham.

Forrest, another lieutenant, and King, the master-at-arms, were on a spar, very much exhausted—Forrest so much so that he murmured, "Don't touch me—I'm too far gone!"

We picked up a man, a leading stoker, who had got under a spar, and was being rolled round and round with it. The spar was on his chest, and the ducking would soon have drowned him if we had not pulled him into the boat.

Our clumsy boat was by this time drifting farther and farther astern, and as we could not see any other survivor floating about, we dropped our anchor, and Watts, the dear old master—a rank now replaced by that of navigating lieutenant—suggested that we should offer a prayer for our deliverance.

He himself recited aloud the Lord's Prayer and the Prayer for those at Sea—which were probably all that anybody could recall at such a time. Watts still enjoys an honoured old age, after being master of the Queen's yacht and Staff Captain of Portsmouth Dockyard.

We had a very mixed crew in our boat of about 100. Many people had got into her off the *Bombay*'s stern. Amongst them was a middy—Stevenson—a light weight luckily, who, in his hurry, jumped off the taffrail, first pitching his sextant down. The height could not have been less than thirty feet, and he alighted on the heads of those who were in the boat. Wonderful to relate, he did no damage—perhaps because the heads were so close together.

I only saw one jump taken, but it was a very sad attempt. One poor fellow, who was in the boat which we did not manage to hoist out, leapt out of her when the smoke became unbearably thick, but instead of alighting on the deck, he went plump down a hatchway covered with a tarpaulin, into the heart of the fire, and must have been destroyed instantly.

He was one of the few who perished inside the ship; we only knew certainly of two others—men who said they would go and try to save some of their valuables. They went below and were never seen again. Nothing could live in such a furnace.

Falling anchors, spars, etc., killed several men under the bows, but the bulk of the 92 who were lost were drowned because of their inability to swim. Having anchored our boat when we found that there were no more lives to save, we got her to rights. Those who had been lucky enough to escape with their clothes on, lent some of their garments to the less fortunate survivors, of whom a number were naked.

The three masts had by this time fallen, and the hull was rapidly burning down. Still, to our wonder, neither of the magazines blew up. The smaller boats had all clustered ahead of the ship, and after distributing their cargoes, volunteers were called for to save those who were still clinging under the bows.

These volunteers instantly came forward and made two most hazardous trips, and safely took off all who had not been carried down by falling wreckage. These rescued men were unable to swim, and Stirling, who was amongst them, saw many a poor fellow sink.

Among other risks of this undertaking was that of encountering a stream of molten lead which the intense heat was causing to run from the bows, and the marks of which were left on more than one survivor.

On this dangerous service, which was carried out in the most gallant fashion, Mandeville, then a sub-lieutenant, greatly distinguished himself. He was specially promoted for this service, and the commander was also specially promoted for his conduct.

So incredibly fast had the flames taken possession of the whole ship that certainly within an hour of the outbreak the mainmast had fallen, and it can hardly have been more than half that time before we were driven out of her, having hoisted out all our boats but one.

It was now about six o'clock, and getting dark and cold, too, so that I was very glad to have a shirt from one of the dry men and to put my legs through the sleeves for trowsers, my own soaked flannel and shirt having been till then my only garments.

The pinnace had been relieved of part of her immense cargo of 150 men by a pilot boat—she was so seriously overladen that she was only kept afloat by the men making an extra gunwale with their backs, and so keeping the water, or rather the slop, out.

It was lucky, indeed, therefore, that the pilot boat, which had been hovering about, came and took some of the people out of her. We communicated with the pinnace and divided our store of small masts and sails which we had picked up, thrown from the boats ahead, and then made sail for Monte Video, which we could see in the distance, fifteen miles off. We used blankets, bed covers, awnings, and anything else we could lay hands on as sails.

All Monte Video was astir by this time, and ship after ship of various nations came tearing out. There were three sailing ships in sight: an English brig called the *Water Lily,* which came down to windward and hove to among the small boats ahead; a Hanoverian brig, which was standing out from inshore; and the French ship, but she was a long way to leeward, although beating up towards us.

The ships were too late to help in saving life; but they put us sooner into safety, for our heavily laden boats would ill have stood the sort of sea that gets up so quickly in those shallow waters, and which, as a matter of fact, swiftly followed our landing.

The pinnace and our own boat were picked up by a passenger steamer, the *Rio de la Plata,* which was just starting for Buenos Ayres. She was really a mailboat, and we were very glad to get on board, especially as a Brazilian steamer had calmly steamed past without taking any notice of our distress or offering help. We went below into the saloon and had some grog, and glad enough we were of it; but we were soon driven out by the entrance of a host of ladies who had come to dinner. Our rig was not suitable for mixed company.

We went on deck, and were just up in time to see the last of the *Bombay*. There was, at each end of her, as I have explained, a magazine containing some forty tons of powder. We could not have believed it possible that their walls of wood and mortar could have so long resisted the furnace they were in. Just five hours had passed since the discovery of the fire under the after magazine, and it is marvellous that the ship escaped so long.

Suddenly we saw a fan-shaped flame shoot up from the dull red spot where the *Bombay* was burning, then ten miles from us. In two minutes there was total darkness, and everything that was left of our home and its contents, as well as all we owned, was buried under muddy waters of the river Plate. This was about 8:30 P.M.

When we got into Monte Video, as all our own ships had gone out, we proceeded to the French storeship *Fortune,* and our friends the French, with whom we were on most excellent terms at that station, overwhelmed us with kindnesses, from the admiral downwards.

The admiral—he was an enormously stout old gentleman— gave me one of his shirts, which I kept for many years. The captain of the *Rio de la Plata* presented me with a pair of trousers—he must, like many others, have given away all his kit—and we were clothed and fed and looked after in the most generous fashion. A large part of us, indeed, were put up for a week by our French friends on board their ships, and some also by the Italian frigate *Regine*.

We mustered the crews of the launch and the pinnace, and found that in these two boats alone we had no fewer than 180 men. We could have taken a great many more in the launch, but the pinnace was chock full.

The *Stromboli,* our largest remaining vessel, with the admiral and his staff on board, came in about eleven o'clock. At midnight we went on board her, and roughly estimated that ninety of our number were missing. This proved to be nearly correct, the actual number being ninety-two, including a couple of officers—Smallhorn, the surgeon, and Franklin, the boatswain—who were lost under the *Bombay's* bows, and some fifteen seamen. The rest were marines, etc.

Dr. Smallhorn's death was as tragic as it was remarkable. He was a non-swimmer, and, like most of those who were similarly helpless, he was watching and waiting for a chance to escape by being taken off in one of the boats. He was sitting on the sheet anchor, outside the ship, when it was burnt from its securing chains, and he went to the bottom with the great mass of iron which formed the anchor.

Early on the morning after the disaster, Stirling and Skinner, a midshipman, were sent home by the French mailboat to report the disaster, the news of which was telegraphed to England from Lisbon—in those days the nearest cable station.

I was ordered to take a party of fifty men to the Lamport and Holt steamer *Herschel,* which had been chartered to bring us home, to clear her lower deck of hides and bones, and otherwise prepare her for our reception.

We left Monte Video in a week's time for England, and on our way out passed the scene of our disaster. The *Bombay's* bowsprit, held by its wire rigging, was bobbing awash, the ship having sunk in only seven fathoms—forty-two feet—of water. Even that soon disappeared, and what had been a noble battleship was covered by the mud.

We picked up one body and buried it. This was the only

one that was ever heard of, for, strangely enough, no corpses went ashore.

On the passage home every effort was made to find some reason for the fire, and the court martial by which we were all tried got no further towards a solution of the mystery. Not one of the survivors has been able to offer a satisfactory suggestion on the point.

The story is not complete without the finding of the court martial, the effect of which was as follows:

That after five days' investigation the Court was of opinion that no evidence had been given by which the origin of the fire could be traced, and that Captain Campbell, and the other officers, and the crew of Her Majesty's late ship *Bombay* were not to blame.

The Court therefore acquitted Captain Campbell, his officers, and crew of all blame.

The Court considered it a duty to call the attention of the Lord Commissioners of the Admiralty to the many instances of heroism and devotion exhibited by the officers and men of the *Bombay* in the numerous cases that had been mentioned in the evidence, and to say that the examples set by all the officers must have contributed largely to the saving of so many lives.

CHAPTER 13

The *Starry Crown*

The last time I corresponded with the great explorer, Vilhjalmur Stefansson, was when I received a letter in Norwegian from Peder Naesheim of the *Rogalands Avis,* a newspaper of Norway. Mr. Stefansson translated the letter which had appeared in the Norwegian paper. On February 6, 1962, I published the story and its translation in my column in the *Patriot Ledger* of Quincy, Massachusetts.

On an earlier occasion Vilhjalmur Stefansson had fascinated me with a weird tale of the Antarctic, an incredible account which he had heard years before. He explained to me how a Norwegian named Bull was the first man to go ashore at Antarctica, and then went on to tell of a craft named *Starry Crown.*

"The tale I cannot prove," explained Stefansson, "but you may use it any way you wish. Nevertheless, I will not give it to you unless you make it clear that it may just as well be a legend as the truth!"

Far away in the Antarctic, frozen into the ice, still lies a famous clipper, the *Starry Crown*. Aboard her is a treasure of gold. It has been said that in olden days people believed that lost treasure was guarded by demons so that those who sought it did so at great risk. If ever an account of lost gold bore out this belief it is the story of the *Starry Crown*.

In the year 1875 the *Starry Crown* was a fine clipper of sixteen hundred tons burden. She left Melbourne for London with a valuable cargo of Australian gold. Never reaching port, she was given up as lost, becoming one of the many unsolved mysteries of the sea.

Twenty years later the whaler *Swordfish* sailed out of Hobart, Tasmania. After a six months' cruise she started homeward with a good cargo of oil, but relentless storms from the north pushed her back against the pack ice.

The grinding pack shifted around the *Swordfish*, sending her deeper and deeper into the frozen wastes, and she was soon helplessly imprisoned with her human cargo. Weeks went by. Food became scarce, and then the men started to come down with scurvy.

Scurvy can easily be cured with the proper remedies, but the lime juice aboard the *Swordfish* had run out, and there were no fresh fruits and vegetables. Even the medicine began to run low. The first to get the illness was the captain, who grew worse and died. One by one the others passed away until at last the only survivors were the first mate, a man called Roland Last, and four sailors. Mate Last, being the only officer left alive, thus became the master of the *Swordfish*.

One morning Captain Last climbed painfully to the masthead to take his regular daily observation of the surrounding masses of ice. Suddenly he caught sight of a ship's royal yards and topgallant masts looming over the top of a great square berg which appeared to be grounded. As the pack bore the *Swordfish* slowly beyond the big iceberg, there came into sight a large full-rigged ship, her masts and rigging still standing and her sails furled. Frozen in hard and fast and lying with a slight list to starboard, she was protected from the pack by two gigantic grounded bergs.

Speechless with excitement, Last stared at the apparition. Then, after shaking his head to see if he might be dreaming, he shouted down to the other survivors.

"Ship to the south. It looks like an old-timer."

Climbing down as rapidly as possible, he grabbed his companions and danced around the deck. As their vessel drifted closer, the four men stared at the ship in amazement. Presently they were able to see the name painted on her bows, *Starry Crown.*

"If we could only get over to her!" Last groaned. "Should there be lime juice, medicines and provisions aboard and we could get them over here, it might mean the difference between life and death. Who'll come with me for a try at it?"

Since there was only one man strong enough for the venture, he and Captain Last attempted the trip. For the moment the drift had ceased, and the *Swordfish* remained motionless. No one could tell when she would begin to move again, but the chance of obtaining medicine and provisions made the risk seem worthwhile. Letting themselves down the side of the ship, the pair took their bearings and then clambered clumsily across the piled floes until they succeeded in reaching the *Starry Crown.* Speed was essential if they were to return before their ship started off again, and so they climbed aboard and quickly explored the clipper ship from stem to stern. The whole vessel was in excellent order, the only things missing being the usual number of boats. Only one of these was left.

In the galley they found a substantial amount of frozen lime juice and quantities of other food of all types. How much could they carry? What was most essential? They finally decided on lime juice and medicines, which they stored ready to grab as they left the ship. But first they must look in the hold. When they went below, they were startled to discover 122 chests of Australian gold with unbroken seals!

Suddenly, as they were about to pry open one of the chests, the ice pack gave a great, crunching groan. Captain Last realized that they would have to return to the *Swordfish* at once or they might meet the same fate as the crew of the *Starry Crown*. Grabbing the supplies, they hurried back to their craft and reached her just in time, for a southwesterly gale had sprung up and the whole pack was moving again, pushing them toward the open sea.

Driven north, the whaler was ground along in the pack day after day, with the men expecting the *Swordfish* to sink at any moment. The wind continued to blow from a southerly point, and finally they found themselves once more in open water. By this time the *Swordfish* was a wreck, leaking fast from the battering she had received from the ice floes. The survivors believed that they had merely exchanged one form of death for another. One particular leak abaft the house was causing the most trouble, as it was increasing by the hour. Soon both pumps were unable to contain the water, and slowly the depth in the hold rose. Then, when the end seemed almost certain, the men sighted another ship. She was the *Nereus*, sailing from Cape Town to Melbourne.

The five men were transferred at the last possible moment, just as their vessel was about to founder. Before the *Nereus* resumed her voyage, the ill-fated *Swordfish* disappeared beneath the waves.

The five survivors all became violently ill, and Captain Last watched as his four companions grew worse and died, to be buried at sea. By the time the *Nereus* sailed into Melbourne Harbor, Last had decided to return to the Arctic and take away the great treasure from the *Starry Crown*. He realized that he was the only man alive who knew that the clipper ship with all her gold was still above water. He also felt sure that she was likely to remain in the ice forever.

Last kept the secret locked in his breast for several years. Then he became mate under Captain Arnold Manton. As he grew to know his captain better, he decided to tell him his secret. When Last ended his story, Captain Manton stared at him quietly for several minutes. Then he spoke.

"Where was the *Starry Crown* when you last saw her?"

"I made a carefully drawn map of the area."

"I'll give you my decision in the morning."

When morning came Manton was ready with his decision —he would go. His ship, the *Black Dog*, was overhauled. Then, with Last serving as mate, the *Black Dog* left Port Phillip Heads, eventually reaching Bass Straits and finally the latitude of the *Starry Crown,* although still a little west of their goal.

The next morning the ship entered an ice floe. Soon she was trapped by a jam, and before anyone realized it, was caught by a heavy berg. Last realized unhappily that the *Black Dog* would be crushed between the berg and the floe.

Leaping into the sea, Last and Manton managed to get on

the floe. They watched as the berg struck the *Black Dog* and pushed her broadside against the floe, and the stout timbers of the craft were crushed as if they were paper. Ten minutes later the *Black Dog* had gone down, taking with her every other sailor aboard.

The two discouraged men decided there was nothing left to do but hike across the floe in the general direction of the place where Last had visited the *Starry Crown*.

Hour after hour they clambered along, sometimes high on a great pressure ridge, on other occasions forced to walk for miles around bergs impossible to climb. Finally Last began to feel the effects of his long struggle over the ice, and a deadly drowsiness came over him. Three times he staggered and fell, and Manton took the lead.

Manton now climbed a high ridge, leaving Last to rest. Once on the top, Manton sighted far in the distance what was apparently their goal. It was a clipper ship, and he easily made out her royal yards. Indeed it was a full-rigged clipper, with her sails furled. Her rigging was still standing, and she was frozen in the ice.

"There she is," he shouted, "about a mile away!"

Both men took heart from the discovery, but found the *Starry Crown* was more nearly five miles away than the mile Manton had estimated.

Three hours later they climbed aboard and went at once to the pantry, where they opened tins of biscuits and bottles of wine. Lighting a fire, they placed a kettle of snow on the galley stove. Manton discovered a tin of coffee, some condensed milk and a package of sugar. They drank the coffee with delight, Last stating years later that it was the best he had ever tasted. Warmed by the galley stove and with full stomachs, the men entered the captain's cabin, found some blankets and fell asleep in the bunks.

Twenty-four hours later Last and Manton awakened. The sixty-year-old ship which had been in the Antarctic wastes for forty-seven years was still in a good state of preservation. There was enough food to last for years.

Last chose the following day to take Captain Manton down in the hold and show him the gold. It was packed in chests of four bars each. There was 2,050 pounds in all, totaling in value more than $1,000,000. Unfortunately, from the moment when Manton viewed this fortune he was unable to think clearly on any other subject, for his mind was dominated by the treasure.

With the arrival of stormy weather there was little to do. Last, because of his experience in whalers, stood it well, and at first he and Manton got along. They shared the cabin, and took turns cooking and tidying up. Then one day Last noticed that Manton would often sit still for hours, staring into space. On rare occasions when he did talk it was of gold.

One day he announced that the wealth should be brought out of the hold and divided. Finally Last agreed. They went down into the hold and carried the chests one by one to the cabin, where they smashed them open. Manton insisted that the golden bars would have to be stacked in two equal piles, but he did not stop when the stacks were complete. On the very next day he carried his share of the gold into another cabin and locked it there.

After that, according to Last, Manton became very peculiar, but of course it is possible the captain had the same thought about his mate. Following a few well-chosen words, the two men decided to sleep in separate cabins.

Then the day came when Manton refused to leave his cabin. Last told him that breakfast was ready, but Manton did not answer. The mate now believed that his captain's mind was giving away, for he could hear Manton muttering to himself. Finally Manton would neither eat nor speak, but managed to get possession of one of two revolvers which they had found in the ship. Last decided that Manton was now a dangerous maniac, and began carrying the other revolver with him constantly.

One terrible night, at the height of a hurricane, Last watched with horror as his cabin door began to open. Then he saw Manton's face, which was contorted beyond reason. The captain held a lamp in his left hand and the pistol in his right. The gun was leveled at Last's head. Snatching his own revolver from under the pillow, Last fired. Reeling away, Manton fell with a crash and died at once.

Filled with horror, Last realized that he had killed the man whom he had induced to embark on the treasure quest! The next day he buried his friend, reading a service from a prayer book aboard the clipper. Carving Manton's name and age on a board, he fastened it on the grave.

Then followed an overwhelming loneliness, so terrible that Last was always reluctant to talk about it afterward. Gradually the days began to grow longer and the weather improved. The mate now set to work building a sledge. When it was finished, he put a small boat aboard the sledge and loaded it with provisions, but he came to what might be regarded as a strange decision regarding the gold. Not one bar of the treasure for which the expedition was formed would he take with him. It was now eight months that he had spent on the *Starry Crown,* and he left the ship in fine, mild weather.

Reaching open water three days later, he changed to the skiff and began rowing northward. On the second day out he sighted a three-masted schooner, which proved to be the *Spray,* (Captain Harmer), and was soon aboard. Last told his rescuers that he was the only survivor of the *Black Dog.* He never mentioned the *Starry Crown* or the treasure.

A few weeks later he landed at Melbourne, but never went back for another try at the golden treasure. Although scores of planes have flown over the last-reported location of the *Starry Crown,* she has not been sighted, and the ship of gold will possibly remain one of the great mysteries of the frozen wastes.

CHAPTER 14

Derelict

A derelict at sea fascinates landlubbers and sailors alike. Abandoned vessels are carefully reported when they are seen, and every effort is made to rid the oceans of these terrible menaces. In one year the U. S. Coast Guard patrol destroyed no less than forty-eight derelicts, but, of course, that was more than half a century ago when sailing vessels were much more common than they are today.

Scores of so-called derelicts have drifted ashore at Sable Island, mentioned in another chapter, and it is said that the Sargasso Sea often catches many of these abandoned craft.

A typical example of a derelict is the coal steamer *Dunmore*. On January 19, 1906, the *Dunmore* was abandoned by her crew in mid-Atlantic because it was feared that she would sink at any moment. After her crew left her, the obstinate *Dunmore* remained afloat. In the next month and a half sixteen vessels sighted her. One liner, the *St. Louis,* had a narrow escape, altering her course in the nick of time to prevent crashing into the wreck. A vessel from the West Indian squadron was the next to sight the *Dunmore* and, with gunfire, sent this unusual derelict to the bottom.

About the year 1870 a dangerous derelict was sighted off the coast of Maine. The cruiser *Atlanta* fired a torpedo into her, but she did not sink. Two more torpedoes were fired with no effect either. The captain of the *Atlanta* then reversed his engines and prepared to ram. Steaming into the abandoned craft, the *Atlanta* hit her square amidships and sent her straight to the bottom. Unfortunately, a large part of the *Atlanta*'s bow broke off and went down with the derelict. Had the sea been rough, the warship might also have gone to the bottom, but she steamed for Boston, where she was dry-docked and repaired.

On January 28, 1899, the English bark *Siddartha* sailed from Jacksonville, Florida. Running into a bad gale, she was abandoned at sea in a waterlogged condition. The *Siddartha* became one of the most famous derelicts of all time, sighted on no less than fifty-seven occasions while drifting at sea. Three attempts were made to set fire to her and send her to the bottom, but she refused to sink. Finally, a British warship was able to destroy her.

The *Ada Cummings,* which floated around the North Atlantic for 549 days, was another derelict ship which attracted a great amount of attention. From her abandonment off New Jersey, she drifted across the ocean almost to Ireland, then came down to a point off Portugal and floated out into the Sargasso Sea. After coming ashore on the coast of Columbia, South America, she was broken up there.

One craft has the unusual record of going adrift as a derelict twice! In October, 1905, the Swedish bark *Orion* was picked up at sea by the steamer *Exeter City* and brought into Halifax. Renamed, she sailed out under the British flag. When she was abandoned in a storm a year later, she was sighted and recognized as a derelict by an American warship which was able to sink her with one torpedo.

The world's record for length of time as a derelict at sea is held by the *Fanny Wolston*. Abandoned in mid-Atlantic, she was seen later off New York and then was sighted in the Gulf of Mexico. Set afire on several occasions, she simply refused to sink. From the time of her abandonment until she was last sighted, no less than 1,408 days had elapsed.

Possibly the most unusual incident connected with the abandonment of a ship happened to the crew of the *John Blake,* who fled their craft off Cuba in the year 1885. While the men were rowing to land in the boats, they sighted a ship lying on a sand bar—actually another derelict. Getting her off the shoal, they sailed her all the distance to England, where they were awarded salvage for their services.

Of course, the most celebrated case of the abandonment of a craft was that of the *Mary Celeste,* about which I have written in several books. In 1872 she was found in good condition off the shores of the Iberian Peninsula and was brought into Gibraltar by a prize crew.

The actual story of the sighting and the boarding of another derelict has been given me by Captain Walter E. Scott of Bucksport, Maine. It is told as follows in the diary of Charles Dixon, the chief officer on the merchant ship *Erin's Isle:*

Sunday, November 17th, 1901.
Position at noon—Latitude 29° 30′ south, Longitude 23° 30′ west.

There has been a light breeze from the north west all day with a heavily-clouded sky, and a long, heavy swell from the westward.

Until 1:30 P.M. today everything went on as usual on a fine Sunday. The wind being steady there was no work to do, so most of the watch were sitting in various shady corners about the deck, reading. I was sitting on that part of the quarterdeck where I could have a view of all that was going on, and also ahead of the vessel, reading one of Max Pemberton's most interesting stories, when I happened to look up, and about nine miles ahead was what appeared to be a steamer bound to the eastward.

I thought it rather strange to see a steamer here, as we were quite out of the track of steamers; so I went and got the telescope, and on looking at her through this saw at once it was not a steamer, but a dismasted ship, and to all appearances in ballast and without any sign of life on board. I told the boatswain, who had seen it by this time, and who was standing at the front of the poop deck, what it appeared to be.

The apparently abandoned vessel was two points on the starboard bow, so that if we kept our course we should pass it at a distance of about a mile and a half or two miles. I then went down in the cabin to notify the captain (who was having his afternoon doze) of what was in sight, and that if he wished to find out all about her we should have to alter our course. He told me at once to alter the course so as to pass close to the dismasted vessel. I went on deck and did as was required, and in a few moments the captain came up and we both had a good look through the glasses, but, although we were then a little nearer than when we first sighted her, we could make out no more than I had at first.

By this time it had spread through the ship that there was something unusual in sight, and everyone on board, even the watch below, who were a few moments ago sound asleep, were up on the forecastle head deck, dressed in whatever articles of clothing had come to hand first when jumping out of their bunks—and some of them had not stopped to get much. Everyone was gazing anxiously and expectantly at the mystery.

But our curiosity was not to be satisfied for some time. The wind, which had been but a light breeze all day, fell away until at times it was almost a calm, the ship moving along at about two miles an hour, and the object of our curiosity was still some eight miles distant. When it fell nearly calm our impatience to solve this mystery caused the use of rather stronger language (when speaking of the wind) than was suitable for Sunday.

However, the time began to pass faster when we began to argue and speculate as to the cause of the wreck's present condition; whether the masts had been cut away to save the vessel, or whether a sudden squall had dismasted her; or was she burnt out?

Then, again, was there anything of value on board? Could she be rigged up and taken to the nearest port to be refitted or sold. And some of us had got so far that we were planning how to spend our share of the salvage money.

And then the question arose, what had become of the crew? Had they been killed in the disaster which had befallen the ship, or had they left in boats or been taken off by a passing vessel, or were they still on board? These and a hundred other speculations kept us busy talking until 4:15 P.M. We were then about a mile and half from the wreck, and it could easily be seen that she was an iron vessel and had been but recently in dock, as the paint on the hull was fresh and clean. But that was all we could discover, as she was lying over very much and had the high side towards us, so that we could not get a glimpse of her deck.

It was now almost a calm, so the captain decided to put out the small boat at once, as it was getting late in the day and we could row much faster than the ship was then going. So the boat was put out and three men and myself jumped into her and we left our ship. About a quarter to five we were up to the wreck. In passing under her stern we read the name, the *Norfolk Island*, of Glasgow. As we pulled around to the lee side so that we could get a view of the deck, it nearly took my breath away to see such a sight; the other side had looked so promising. She had been completely burnt out, so as to be useless, and apparently had not a thing of value on her.

However, we determined to go on board. So we pulled cautiously to the vessel, keeping a sharp look-out for any sunken wreckage that might sink the boat, but there was none, and we got safely alongside. I seized hold of one of the shrouds that was hanging over the side and climbed on board. One of the others soon followed.

The fire had done its work only too well. There was not a vestige of woodwork to be seen; nothing but bent and twisted iron beams, the broken bulwarks, and the remains of the shattered masts. In the bottom of the vessel was a rather strange combination of elements. In the after part there was about 100 to 150 tons of coal and cinders still smouldering. In the forward part was water about three or four feet deep.

The vessel had been loaded with coal, and was of about 2200 tons burden.

We first went aft, where the cabin had been, and here apparently the fire had not been so fierce as elsewhere. Amongst the ashes I noticed many articles that had been used in the cabin. One of the first things I noticed was the works of the cabin clock, with the hands still attached, and stopped at

three o'clock; also the ship's bell, which I secured as a me-
mento of our visit; also all the tins in which the cabin stores
had been, and many things to remind one that it had once
been the habitation of men of whose fate we were ignorant.
We then went along to where the cook house had been, and
here found that, owing to its being protected from the direct
heat of the burning cargo by an iron deck, nearly everything
was intact; that is, the stove and most of the cooking utensils. I
then went down into the after hold on the top of the smouldering coal. But it was rather too hot and stifling to stay. I
then climbed into the 'tween decks and there took a photo.
I then climbed on the upper deck, and after that the other
man and I climbed pretty well all over the vessel to see if
there were anything of value to be found; and it was climbing, with the deck beams at an angle of about forty degrees
and the vessel rolling so that at times the deck seemed nearly
perpendicular.

There was nothing to crawl about on except the deck
beams, which were about eight inches wide; and when in the
middle of one there was the prospect that when the ship
lurched one might drop comfortably among a tangled mass
of iron and wire and cinders, some twenty-two feet below. I
think the knowing that we might never have the chance of
boarding a derelict again made us feel that we wanted to see
all that was to be seen, and to experience to the full what it
was like to be on board an abandoned vessel, as it is an experience that very few have had.

While I was down in the hold of the vessel I tried to realize
the sensations of one left alone on a vessel in this state. I was
out of sight of our own ship and could not see the man who
had come on board the wreck with me. There were heavy
clouds in the sky, which at that time of day made it very
gloomy. Add to this the mournful sound made by the uncon-

trolled rudder moving with the sea, the washing backward and forward of the water in the hold, together with a peculiar moaning sound as of someone in agony, made by the remains of the masts moving slowly as the vessel rolled.

With these surroundings, and when I realized how helpless a human being would be in such a position, there came over me a feeling of such despair and hopelessness as I never again wish to experience. Everything seemed so real that I can hardly say how relieved I felt, when I climbed on deck, to see our boat waiting to take me to the ship, where we should have cheerful surroundings, the companionship of a few of our fellow men, and a sense of security not to be felt on board the derelict of the good ship *Norfolk Island*.

One of the most curious things I noticed on board, close to the foremast where it was broken off at the side of the ship, was a piece of sail caught on the bulwarks, where even the iron was bent with heat. How the canvas was not consumed is more than I can solve, and I have given it serious thought. Someone might offer a suggestion. I wish they would for there is something uncanny in the thing which worries me. There was also a wooden pulley in the same place, also intact. It was the only piece of wood in the ship that had not been burnt. Within three inches of where the pulley lay the deck planks were completely destroyed.

It was now nearly half past five, and although the sun was still above the horizon the sky was so heavily clouded that it was quite dark, and as there was nothing to be gained by remaining longer I called the men left in charge of the boat. They came alongside and we started for our own vessel, then about a mile and a half away, where we arrived about 6 P.M.

After hoisting in the boat we at once imparted all the news we had to tell, the facts that demolished all the castles in the air we had built while approaching this abandoned vessel;

now we were leaving her, and although we knew something concerning her we were still ignorant of the fate of the crew. Probably we shall find out that when we arrive in Cape Town, if they have been picked up by another vessel.

About 7 P.M. we saw the last of the *Norfolk Island*. As she faded from our sight in the gathering mists of evening she presented a picture of such desolation that it left an impression to be long remembered as a fitting close to an incident that is likely to remain unique in the writer's seafaring career.

When Charles Dixon reached Cape Town he learned of the crew of the *Norfolk Island*. On October 23, 1901, the London *Daily Graphic* had printed the following story about them:

Terrible tales of suffering and privation at sea were told yesterday by members of two shipwrecked crews brought home to England by the R.M.S. *Thames*. . . . One party consisted of survivors of the British Barque *Norfolk Island,* which left Leith Roads on July 6th, bound for Cape Town, with a cargo of coal. Towards the end of August it was found that the cargo was getting heated. Everything possible was done by the officers and men to save the ship, but an explosion took place on September 5th, and the crew escaped in two boats. In the darkness they drifted out of each other's sight, one boat being at sea twelve and the other fourteen days before they were picked up. The crew, who belonged to Leith, Cardiff, Carnarvon, and Portmadoc, were landed at Bahia, whence they were sent home by the British consul little the worse for their adventure.

The fate of the derelict *Norfolk Island* will always remain one of the unsolved mysteries of the sea. Some believe that wreckage which came ashore at Tristan de Cunha, 800 miles from the place where the *Erin's Isle* last saw her, was from the *Norfolk Island,* but, of course, this is pure conjecture. No one will ever really know.

CHAPTER 15

An Infernal Machine

If the casual visitor to Boston approaches the area on the water front near the corner of State Street and Atlantic Avenue and faces east, he may view the site of the Old Salt House at Long Wharf, the building in which Nathaniel Hawthorne is said to have written part of his *Scarlet Letter.* To me it also recalls William Kellogg Thompson, who was a man without a conscience. When the row of buildings including the Salt House was torn down some years ago, with it went all physical evidence of what was the scene of the planning of one of the most diabolical crimes ever carried out against human beings.*

On a pleasant September day in 1905 William Kellogg Thompson landed in Boston from England. He went at once

---

* Many of the details of the Boston part of this story were told to me years ago by Captain Lawrence H. Dunn, Harbor Master of the City of Boston.

on a tour of the water front and found what he was after in the third-floor loft of the Old Salt House. There he hired three rooms in which, he told the landlord, he was anxious to conduct experiments. In this manner the staid old city of Boston received one of her most nefarious guests.

Becoming well-known in the water-front district, Thompson was often seen at noontime down on nearby T Wharf. A harmless-looking young man in his early thirties, he was apparently enjoying with scores of others the privilege of looking out across Boston Harbor as part of his optional noontime relaxation.

Nevertheless, underneath Thompson's pleasant manner and smiling countenance there lurked a cunning, murderous mind. Even then Thompson was carrying out the first part of a scheme which would result in the wholesale destruction of many of his fellow men. As the weeks went by, up in the three rooms of the Old Salt House loft, he was slowly building an infernal machine.

One night, however, as Thompson worked on his experiment, something went wrong which could not be kept a secret. The first the outside world knew of Thompson's trouble was when the policeman on the beat, Patrolman Leslie by name, started walking toward the Atlantic Avenue water front.

Suddenly the earth shook around him, followed almost at once by a dull, muffled explosion. The noise of shattering glass then came to him from far in the distance. Breaking into a run, Leslie soon reached the Long Wharf area where he could see clouds of smoke pouring from the shattered third-floor loft windows of the Old Salt House. After running up the stairs, Leslie tried to force open the door, but it was locked. Battering his shoulder against the heavy oak barrier, he finally forced it open on his third try.

There, stretched out on the loft floor, was William Thompson, his unconscious form splattered with plaster, chemicals, and blood. His workshop was a shambles; broken graduates, beakers, bottles, and chemical supplies littered the room. Giving the man first aid, Leslie pulled Thompson to a nearby cot where he loosened his collar. A few minutes later Thompson recovered consciousness and grinned sheepishly as he realized what had happened.

Patrolman Leslie now whipped out his notebook and began questioning Thompson: "Well, now, what's all this about?"

"I'm sorry, sir, but I use this loft in my experiments. I was working tonight on an invention which I hoped would give me a living. It is a plan to feed ship's lights automatically. Evidently something has gone wrong with my calculations."

"There's no doubt about that," retorted the policeman, "for I heard the explosion over on Milk Street. Why, man, you could kill yourself that way very easily."

Thompson smiled again, but remained silent.

Patrolman Leslie finished writing his report, admonished Thompson to be more careful in the future, and left the building.

Once he was certain that Leslie had gone, Thompson made feverish plans for his own departure. When dawn came stealing across Boston Bay he had all his materials, tools, and chemicals packed and ready. Making sure that he was equal to the trip, he went up into the fruit and produce market, hired a pushcart man and guided him down to the Old Salt House. By seven o'clock everything pertaining to William

Kellogg Thompson had vanished from the area. He and the pushcart man reached South Boston. Within a short time he had engaged another loft above an old unused stable on D Street, where he set up his workbench again. Within a few weeks he had made final arrangements to construct another machine.

Later that month a large case about four feet square arrived at the loft. Thompson had the expressmen carry it up the two flights to the third floor, for it was very heavy.

During the next two weeks Thompson was so busy he scarcely took time to go out for lunch. Finally he completed his arrangements and called the draymen to ship the machine to New York. It was a tremendous task for the movers to get the heavy metal invention down the stairs, but after much bumping, banging, grunting, and cursing, the case was put aboard the dray, and two hours later was bound for New York City.

With the shipment of the package Thompson concluded his arrangements in South Boston and took the next train for New York. He never returned to Boston.

Several days later William Thompson sailed from New York for Liverpool. Reaching that well-known English metropolis, he hired a loft near the water front from a resident named McGinnis, who, because of reverses, was finding his rent hard to pay.

"My name is Thompson," he explained to McGinnis. "I'm an engineer and am working on an invention which I hope will eventually be used in connection with steamships. I want a quiet place to work where I will not be disturbed. In return I'll try not to bother you."

On the following day he moved into his new quarters. A single traveling bag held all his personal effects. Then came a cot, a workbench, boxes of tools, and a case about four feet square which the workmen carried for him with utmost care.

From the moment Thompson moved in he began to work. He stayed at his chosen task from early morning until late at night. Hour after hour Mrs. McGinnis and her children heard him filing, hammering, tapping—all on metal. The noise of his work did not bother them, but their curiosity was aroused. After a week or so they heard a newer, more peculiar noise. It was such a sound as might be made by some tightly wound-up mechanism, the spring of which had been suddenly released to set up an intense whirring. No one came to see Thompson. He seldom went out except late at night or in the early morning to buy something to eat while he worked.

One day after several weeks had gone by all noise in his room stopped for a time. Suddenly the entire house seemed to shudder, followed at once by a great dull boom. Mrs. McGinnis and the children burst out into the street, terribly frightened, but the house was not seriously damaged. When McGinnis rushed up to Thompson's garret he discovered fumes, smoke, and two smashed skylights.

Finding Thompson stunned but conscious, McGinnis made a quick check of the room. In a cupboard he saw strange-looking packages of some soft material, each bundle carefully wrapped. Oily in nature, the stuff had a vile smell. When Thompson had recovered, McGinnis spoke to him.

"What about the skylights? You are an inventor, I know, but you should pay the damage from your invention."

Thompson agreed, and settled at once for the broken windows.

Nevertheless, as he had done in Boston, Thompson made plans to move and by morning was gone! Later it was discovered that he had established a cellar workshop in the dirtiest and most disreputable part of Liverpool. Here he worked at his invention several weeks longer. How he was able to support himself all this time mystified everyone.

Thompson finally succeeded in building a machine exactly as he wanted it, and again he moved out of his quarters. This time, he hired two carts, using the second one exclusively for his invention. He spent much time instructing the drayman, admonishing him against carelessness.

"Drive slowly," he told the workman as he climbed into the seat with him.

The crated material was put on a train for Southampton where it was stored in a warehouse. Thompson stenciled the box, "Glass Antiques. Fragile."

Thompson now attempted a complete change of personality. With money acquired in a manner still unknown, he purchased a wardrobe and signed the register at one of the best hotels in Southampton, taking the name Norman Stevens Winslow of New York City.

After staying at the hotel for a few days, he gradually let it be known that he was an American art dealer who had come to Europe to buy paintings for customers. Having obtained several priceless bits of ancient glassware, he was anxious to ship them to Germany.

Thompson, now known as Winslow, learned the name of a reputable insurance company from the hotel clerk. He contacted the organization, which sent a clerk with Winslow to the warehouse where the box was kept along with four other crates the inventor had stored there.

Not inquiring about what was in the box, the clerk merely recorded the value which Winslow set upon the contents and placed heavy insurance on the box and each of the other crates as well.

The clerk did ask for a glimpse of the contents of one of the boxes, but Winslow explained that the packing was so delicate that he did not want to open it again. Accepting Winslow's statement, he made out the policy, collected the heavy payment on it, and went to his office. Later the clerk who insured the box wondered why Winslow had been reticent about opening it, but he soon dismissed the incident from his mind.

Winslow crossed the Channel with his precious boxes carefully stowed away in an especially reserved space in the hold of the Channel steamer. After reaching Bremerhaven, he stored the crates on the pier and then visited the office of the English insurance company. He now planned to ship all five crates on the steamer *Mosel* to New York and took out costly policies on his entire cargo.

On the day the *Mosel* was to sail, the streets froze until they were solid sheets of ice. At his hotel, Winslow had his precious boxes brought down to the curb to be loaded on two drays which he had engaged. His plan, evidently, was to go aboard the *Mosel* to make sure the crates were loaded and then debark at Southampton, while the ship continued across the ocean.

When the carts arrived on the Bremerhaven wharf, Winslow was already aboard the *Mosel*. As the first dray was backed into position for unloading, the horse lost his footing and began to slip on the ice. A wheel crunched against the granite guard in the street and the dray tipped over. The box marked "Antique Glass" began to slide, and then a terrible explosion occurred.

What followed belongs in the annals of major marine disasters, although the *Mosel* was still moored to the piling. The earth seemed to open up with a hideous roar, and many steerage passengers standing on the pier were blown to pieces. When the dust began to settle, it was seen that the pier had caved in for a distance of thirty-five feet. The quay was covered with dead and dying men and women, the *Mosel* herself was damaged by the explosion, and the drays, their drivers, and the horses had been blown to bits. Ambulances arrived and carried the dying to the local hospitals and the dead to the morgue.

Some time later Winslow was found dying in his cabin. Although he had evidently attempted suicide, he was still alive and was taken to a hospital. Becoming delirious, he revealed in his ravings just enough of the details of his nefarious plans to make the entire affair one of the great unsolved marine mysteries of nautical history.

A sweeping investigation was begun, and as the police developed the history of what was Thompson-Winslow's life, the trail led to a clockmaker in Bernburg by the name of Michaels. This witness readily volunteered his story, since he was in no way connected with what apparently was a mad but profitable scheme.

The entire plan and how it worked will probably always remain obscure. Nevertheless, after studying the case, one almost surely arrives at certain conclusions. Coupled with the explanations of Michaels and the disappearance of two other vessels at sea, conjectures bordering on certainty are possible. However, they are merely conjectures.

Using all available information, I have worked out a theory which may account for Thompson's actions.

The records indicate that Thompson, under more than one alias, purchased several timing machines from the Bernburg clockmaker. During the same period he established himself as a dealer in rare articles of sculpture and painting.

When his first machine arrived, he set it up in a case which he packed with explosives, thus making the crate or box in actuality a diabolically infernal machine. The other insured boxes, shipped as expensive art treasures, would contain only rubbish. The timing mechanism he set to explode when the ship on which it was placed would be at sea. Thus the heavily insured boxes would be lost with the ship, and the companies would pay the insurance.

What proof do I have of this? Absolutely none, but there are many facts which lend themselves to the explanation.

For example, six months after Thompson purchased his first clock mechanism from Michaels, the freighter *Ella* sailed from Liverpool to Hamburg. Thompson had insured several crates holding rubbish which he called "art goods." Some time later interested parties in Hamburg began to make inquiries as to what made the ship so late. Days went by, and then weeks, but no word came of the *Ella*. The anxious owners started a search, but not the slightest trace of her was ever found. Eventually the company was forced to declare that the ship and twenty-two men had vanished in the English Channel. All insurance on freight aboard was paid in full.

The *Ella* was still being talked about when more art goods

were taken aboard the *Scorpio* a year later. Meanwhile, the watchmaker of Bernburg had sold another timing mechanism which he shipped to Cardiff.

The *Scorpio* sailed for Charente with articles of "valuable curios" heavily insured by a Henri Costeau, a French art collector. As with the *Ella*, the *Scorpio* became overdue and finally was reported as missing. Again the shipping world pondered as to what could have happened, for the *Scorpio* also had vanished without a trace.

It seems that several years prior to the *Ella* disaster, Thompson had visited Michaels with plans and specifications for a bit of clockwork, the exact purpose of which Michaels was never able to determine. Thompson explained to him that the clockwork was to be part of an invention, the remainder of which was to be constructed in another country. When Michaels finished the machine, he was greatly impressed by its cleverness. He particularly enjoyed watching the release of a powerful trigger timed to strike at any time up to ten days after it had been wound up.

Michaels fell in love with the machine and decided to construct a duplicate. After the *Mosel* explosion, this duplicate was carefully examined by police inspectors from England. Of course, the inspectors had no proof that the construction of the machine and the explosion were related, but the assumption is that they were.

If Thompson really planned this horrible way of making money, as it appears from the investigation, he must be set down in history as one of the most fiendish schemers of his generation. But, of course, we shall never know for certain.

CHAPTER 16

The *Waratah* Enigma

In November, 1949, I had the pleasure of meeting and talking with Errol Friedmann of South Africa at the newspaper offices of the *Patriot Ledger* in Quincy, Massachusetts. His grandfather, Captain Aron Friedmann, was a South African newspaperman. Errol and I discussed at considerable length the strange disappearance of a great ocean liner, the *Waratah*, about which I wrote briefly in 1948.*

Later I communicated with Captain Friedmann, who lives in Bergvliet, Cape Town, concerning the *Waratah* mystery. His letter of reply follows:

9 Nov. 1959

Dear Mr. Snow:

I thank you for your letter of the 31st ultimo and in response to your request, I am able to give you the following information about the *Waratah*. She was a combined passenger and cargo ship of the Blue Anchor Line, built on the

---

* *Mysteries and Adventures Along the Atlantic Coast,* p. 172.

Clyde, Scotland, and completed in October 1908. She was a twin screw ship, with three decks fore and aft, a displacement of 16,800 tons and up-to-date equipment, except that she carried no wireless installation. The *Waratah* completed her maiden voyage to Australia and back without mishap. On her return Captain Ilbery, her commander, expressed himself well satisfied on the sailing of the ship.

The *Waratah* left London again on the 27 April 1909. Captain Ilbery, all the same officers with one exception, all the engineers except two, signed on again for the second voyage, and the ship's company numbered in all 119. All went well at sea and after an uneventful voyage the *Waratah* arrived safely in Australia. After calling there at several ports, she put out of Adelaide on July the 7th 1909 reaching Durban, South Africa, on the 25th. At Durban she coaled and took in another 248 tons of cargo, making a total cargo load of slightly over 10,000 tons, and put to sea again on the 26th July with 92 passengers on board.

Her next port of call was Cape Town. At about 6 A.M. on the 27th she overhauled a smaller steamer, called *Clan MacIntire,* having a short conversation with her by signal. The *Clan MacIntire* said she was going to London via East London, S. Africa. The *Waratah* told her that she was also sailing to London, via Cape Town, and that all was well. The *Waratah* then passed on and in a few hours had left the other ship very far behind and had also soon slipped behind the horizon and out of sight of the *Clan MacIntire,* who slowly plodded along on her way.

A little later in the day she ran into a heavy head sea and a strong S.W. gale. On the next day it blew a terrible hurricane, described as the most severe within living memory in those waters. No other ship had been in contact with the *Waratah,* after she had left the *Clan MacIntire.*

The days passed. The *Waratah* became due at Cape Town —and then overdue. People began to feel anxious. All ships that arrived from identical routes could give no news of her. The *Waratah* had disappeared as completely and as mysteriously as if she had never existed. The sea seemed to have opened and suddenly swallowed her up. Three warships were sent out to search for the missing liner, and the Blue Anchor Line chartered the *Sabine* which left the Cape on the 11th September and cruised about for 88 days, travelling over 14,000 miles, without any result. No wreckage, no trace of anything was found that could be regarded as possible evidence.

Maybe during that hurricane some tragic, terrible accident supervened, which sent her and her freight of 211 human lives to the bottom of the sea.

A Board of Trade inquiry was held on the 16 Dec. 1910. In the absence of survivors, it took a long time to get evidence from Australia and South Africa and so nearly 18 months had passed since the disaster had taken place. The Court of Inquiry sat for two months. It succeeded in collecting a mass of interesting information, yet when its sessions closed and its finding had been delivered the central mystery still remained unsolved.

Where, when, how and why did the *Waratah* sink? That is a question which nobody could answer. The Court of Inquiry delivered its finding on February the 23rd 1911 as follows: "The ship was lost in a gale of exceptional violence, the first great storm she had encountered, and she capsized, leaving no trace."

As far as I know, these are the actual facts about the *Waratah*.

A. Friedmann

After receiving Captain Friedmann's letter, I did substantial additional research on the unsolved mystery and found many details of interest. I discovered that Captain Ilbery was an experienced sailor who had been employed by his company since 1868. I learned on good authority that although he had told his employers that he was satisfied with her first voyage, later he admitted she had certain features of instability.

Referring to Captain Friedmann's comments on the overhauling of the *Clan MacIntire*, it appears that the *Waratah* would have been noticed again after passing the *Clan MacIntire* had she still been afloat, for the latter craft sighted almost a dozen vessels in the next two days. On the other hand, if the *Waratah* had gone down, other craft should have seen debris on the surface of the ocean, but not a ship reported anything at the time.

The report of a fire at sea on July 27 has complicated the mystery of the disappearance of the *Waratah*. On that day the ship *Harlow*, under the command of Captain John Bruce, was about a mile and a half to two miles off the shores of South Africa. The master saw smoke billowing from a steamer which was at least ten miles behind the *Harlow*, and the smoke was so thick that the vessel appeared on fire. At dusk Captain Bruce identified two masthead lights and a red sidelight astern, coming from the direction where the smoke had been, and assumed that the steamer was drawing closer. Two hours later the lights appeared to be much nearer. Evidently a fast ship was gaining rapidly on the *Harlow*.

Suddenly from astern there were two bright flashes, resembling explosions from the steamer. The lights then vanished, and nothing further developed. Later, when the

Waratah was reported missing, Captain Bruce at once associated what he had seen with her disappearance.

Later that same night of July 27, three hours after Captain Bruce saw the lights and flashes, a Union Castle boat named *Guelph* began to exchange visual signals with another craft never identified in Morse code. The *Guelph* flashed her name to the other ship, which replied. The other's signal lamp was very faint, and all that could be distinguished were the last three letters of the message, T-A-H. On arrival in Natal the captain of the *Guelph* stated that the *Waratah* must have been the vessel whose signals he had tried in vain to record that evening off East London, South Africa.

Another possibility is that either during the gale into which she must have run later on in the day, or in the hurricane which followed the gale, some accident occurred which sent the *Waratah* to the bottom.

In a later discussion of the loss of the *Waratah* the third officer of the steamship *Tottenham* declared that on the following August 11 he sighted human bodies floating in the sea off the South African coast. The location was between Grahamstown and East London, more than 500 miles east of Cape Town. One member of the ship's company had a vivid recollection of looking down into the water just as the body of a little girl attired in a red dressing gown floated by. The second mate of the *Tottenham* also noticed the body, adding that the little girl was wearing a red hood and black stockings. Her knees were bare. The mate also sighted a ship's bunk floating by. The Chinese firemen aboard, peering out of their portholes, were heard later to state that there were many dead persons in the water.

When Captain Cox of the *Tottenham* was told of the floating bodies he put his ship about at once, but, of course, it is hard to return to an exact location at sea. The *Tottenham* reached the general area where the floating objects had been noticed, but did not put a boat over. Captain Cox then decided that what others thought was a girl was really a roll of printing paper, which had a red wrapper around the middle. The chief engineer reported that although he had sighted no bodies, he did see "pieces of what looked like blubber, but no human bodies."

On the same day, however, in the same general latitude and longitude, the steamship *Insizwa* passed through an area where several bodies were said to have been sighted by members of the ship's company.

Regardless of whether or not bodies were actually sighted, it is almost unbelievable that a 16,800-ton vessel should vanish utterly. Heavily loaded with cargo of all sorts and carrying more than two hundred people, it would seem impossible that she could go down without something from her floating away to be recovered by other craft traveling in the same steamship lane.

When several weeks had gone by without the *Waratah* mystery being solved, person after person began to come forward and offer evidence of what they thought had happened. One man declared that he had always known the *Waratah* was not seaworthy, for she pitched and rolled excessively even in calm weather. One of the officers was said to have admitted she was very unstable. It was then claimed that on one occasion the *Waratah* had almost capsized in the dock. Also, her decks had pulled loose in her maiden voyage, it was confidently asserted.

The usual bottle messages that often appear after a marine

disaster now began to be picked up on the coast of Australia, all allegedly from the *Waratah*. One by one the messages were examined, investigated, and officially denounced as forgeries.

Others believed that they had information which would indicate that during the gale-hurricane of July 27–28 the *Waratah* had been damaged, after which she drifted out of the usual shipping lanes and was even then floating toward some South Sea Island.

Possibly the best explanation is that her cargo had shifted in the storm, causing her to capsize, fill, and go down. Others believed that her hatches had not been properly secured. Thus, according to this theory, when the stormy weather hit, the seas poured into the hatches, and eventually she went to the bottom.

Another reason for her disappearance is suggested by the placement of a coal bunker which had been built on her spar deck and destroyed her center of gravity, according to the theory of a group of mariners.

Many men of the sea believe that the *Waratah* did have an excessive roll. On the other hand, all naval architects and designers agreed that regardless of the roll which had developed, she was properly designed and constructed. On five different occasions she passed inspection, first by the builders, then by the owners. After this the Board of Trade, Lloyd's of London, and the immigration authorities placed their seal of approval on the *Waratah*.

Naval architect Robert Steel went on record as saying that no wind or wave could have capsized the liner unless some mishap had already crippled her. Although the experts agreed that the *Waratah* could not capsize under ordinary conditions, they had to admit that they could offer no other explanation of what did happen. One man who testified at the Court of Inquiry indicated it was impossible that the *Waratah* could sink under any conditions. He seemed personally offended that anyone should suggest that the steamer had gone to the bottom. He had no explanation of where she was, however. Regardless of personal viewpoints as to what could not have taken place, something did happen to the ship, and the mystery will probably forever remain unsolved.

Some time after the vanishing of the liner, a letter came to light which had been sent by the owners of the *Waratah* to the builders about the time of the completion of her maiden voyage. In the letter the owners complained that she was not as seaworthy as the *Geelong*, a sister ship in the same Blue Anchor Line. Later Mr. Lund, the line's managing director, admitted that the captain had told him the *Geelong* was a stiffer boat under light trim than the *Waratah*.

Many persons who had been aboard the *Waratah* on her earlier trip testified that they had great misgivings about the safety of the craft. Nevertheless, in all fairness it must be recalled that eighteen months had elapsed between the vanishing of the *Waratah* and the holding of the inquiry, and many sincere people may have had incorrect recollections after more than a year and a half.

Mr. Claude Sawyer had left Sidney on the *Waratah* on June 28, the beginning of her last successful voyage. Almost immediately he had noted an excessive roll and a definite list to starboard. On one occasion when she rolled, she twisted back again with great violence, flinging the passengers around and injuring several of them.

On another afternoon Sawyer was taking a bath. From the slant of the water in the tub he estimated that the ship must

be at an angle of about 45°. He also noted that the *Waratah*
was habitually slow in recovering from pitching. He had
practically decided to leave the ship at Durban, when the
weather calmed down and allowed him to forget his resolution for the time being.

One night he retired around ten o'clock, when the ship
was three days out from Durban. Suddenly, a short time after
midnight, he awakened from a nightmarish dream. A man
garbed in a peculiar costume had stood before him, holding
a long sword in his right hand and a rag covered with blood
in his left. The apparition appeared three times, convincing
Sawyer that he was being warned to leave the ship. He told
several of the other passengers about his dream the next
morning, and when the ship reached Durban he changed
back to his original resolve and went ashore, wiring his wife
that he thought the *Waratah* top-heavy. While in Durban he
told his dream to the Union Castle Lines manager in that
city.

The *Waratah* sailed from Durban without him, and on
July 28, the day after she must have encountered heavy
weather, Sawyer had another dream at a Durban hotel. There
was the great liner sailing through heavy seas, but as the
dream progressed he watched her being approached by a
gigantic wave. The huge billow climbed right over her bow,
causing the ship to roll over on her starboard side and vanish
from sight. It had been a terrible spectacle in his dream, and
it still frightened him even after he awakened.

There were several other people who testified at the hearing regarding the maiden voyage of the *Waratah*. A Professor
Bragg who had sailed from Adelaide recalled that one morning the starboard list was so bad that the water could not run

out of the bath drain. Later, as he understood it, a water ballast tank was filled in order to bring the ship back to an even keel, but her moment of trim was a brief one, as she then listed to port.

A steward named Herbert, who did not make the fatal voyage, admitted that the *Waratah* rolled excessively when he had been aboard earlier. The ship had a definite list on many occasions. He spoke of the movement of the promenade deck on its beams when the ship rolled, and explained how the great bolts broke off, one falling on the baker's head, and volunteered that he could put his finger between the deck planks and the beams where they should have been tightly bolted.

One man talked of his interview with the chief mate, who was also worried about the ship's performance. He suggested that the chief mate leave the *Waratah*. The mate agreed that he should seek another berth, but he did not change in time and went down with the ship.

Regardless of all statements about the *Waratah,* the findings of the Court of Inquiry, made on February 23, 1911, concluded that the *Waratah* capsized and went down in a gale. The court also stated that it was almost compelled to comment unfavorably concerning the owner's failure to ask the captain for a report after her maiden voyage on her stability and behavior at sea.

The fate of the *Waratah* will always remain one of the great unsolved mysteries of the sea.

CHAPTER 17

Kitchener

The mysterious disappearance of Lord Horatio Kitchener, English Secretary of State for War, and the intense pitch of excitement which resulted immediately after the announcement of it in 1916 seem almost unbelievable today.

Of course, England was then at war and all news was being heavily censored. Many facts had been suppressed, and there were those who hinted at the official release of actual falsehoods. As a result no one really knew what to believe and what not to believe. While the world was in such a mood the announcement was made of Lord Kitchener's death. At the time he was the outstanding personality of the entire British Empire, and it was hard to believe that he had perished in a strange, incredible disaster.

In June, 1916, the battle of Jutland had just been fought, the French had resisted the German attacks on Verdun, and apparently the Russians were rallying from their reverses of the previous year.

Because of this, Lord Kitchener decided to accept the czar of Russia's invitation to visit Petrograd. Lord Kitchener realized the importance of his visit to Russia, but as Secretary of State for War, he could not leave Whitehall for any extended period of time. It is said by some that he was just a trifle suspicious of his war cabinet associates and their desire that he should go to Russia.

On June 2 Kitchener sent a telegram to the chief of the British military mission in Russia, Sir John Hanbury Williams, asking, "Would you ascertain . . . if there is any desire that I should not come, in which case I should not think of doing so?"

Sir John, on receipt of the message, went immediately to the czar, who repeated his hope that Lord Kitchener would make a visit to Russia, which he believed would prove beneficial to both countries, and Kitchener decided that he would have to go.

Late Sunday afternoon, June 4, 1916, Kitchener's official group left London. Sir George Arthur later mentioned an unexpected event aboard the train. "Kitchener . . . came back to the platform and said very quietly—and a little sadly—to his friends, 'Look after things while I am away.' As if unable to explain to himself the impulse which had prompted him to have a last word, he quickly regained his seat and looked away out of the window until the train started."

The train rushed north through Scotland, where it was met by a rising wind and heavy rain. On the morning of June 5 he reached Thurso, where a great sea was rolling tremendous breakers onto the shore. The barometer was still dropping, and without question Kitchener would be in for a violent night at sea. He embarked on a destroyer and reached Scapa

Flow, where he had dinner with Admiral Jellicoe aboard the Iron Duke. The admiral spent some time discussing the battle of Jutland, which was only a few days old, and then the party went aboard the 11,000-ton cruiser H.M.S. *Hampshire,* which had been chosen for the sea journey to Archangel.

The moment the passengers reached the deck of the *Hampshire,* she weighed anchor and sailed out to sea. On reaching deep water Kitchener realized that the weather was even worse than indicated in the harbor. Gigantic seas were rolling in, and his ship had difficulty making speed. The cruiser, because of the storm, shaped her course to the west of Pentland Firth to gain shelter from the northeasterly gale then hitting the area. Traveling at full speed her escort of destroyers could not make headway in the hurricane then blowing. Finally they were forced to abandon their escort tactics and return to Scapa Flow, the *Hampshire* continuing her voyage alone.

Shortly after seven thirty that night, the *Hampshire* blew up. At the time it was believed that a U-boat's torpedo had found its mark, but later several survivors were of the opinion the ship had struck a mine. In the short space of fourteen minutes she had gone down a mile and a half offshore between the Brough of Birsay and Marwick Head. Only twelve men escaped.

Lord Kitchener and his party with all the ship's officers had vanished in the sea. England first learned of the disaster from Admiral Jellicoe in the following dispatch:

I have to report with regret that H.M.S. *Hampshire* (Captain Herbert J. Savill, R.N.), with Lord Kitchener and his Staff on board, was sunk last night about 8 P.M. to the west of the Orkneys, either by a mine or torpedo. Four boats were seen by observers to leave the ship. The wind was N.N.E. and heavy seas were running. Patrol vessels and destroyers at once proceeded to the spot, and a party was sent along the coast to search, but only some bodies and a capsized boat have been found up to the present. As the whole shore has been searched from the seaward, I greatly fear that there is little hope of there being any survivors. No report has yet been received from the party on shore. H.M.S. *Hampshire* was on her way to Russia.

When the explosion occurred, Lord Kitchener was in his cabin. It is believed that he made no attempt to enter any of the four boats. Later, on one raft, forty-three bodies were found frozen to death. In the official British government files we read the report of First Class Petty Officer Wilfred Wesson, one of the twelve survivors of the *Hampshire*. He explained that the explosion occurred at eight o'clock that night, while he was on the mess deck. All lights went out.

"While I was waiting with the others on the half-deck an officer came with Lord Kitchener from the captain's cabin. He called out, 'Make room for Lord Kitchener,' and the men opened out to let Lord Kitchener pass. He went on deck and I did not see any more of him."

Hardly had the water closed over Lord Kitchener's head before enigmatic stories were told about him. When we realize that in the year 1916 other unusual stories had been circulated around England, it is easy to see why the Kitchener mystery developed. This was the same period when Englishmen whispered that Prince Louis of Battenburg had been shot in the Tower of London as a traitor, and that tens of thousands of Russian soldiers were passing through England every day. Kitchener was now said to have lost his life as the result of a carefully planned plot. Even today in England I am sure there are still thousands of people who feel that his death was not the result of a German U-boat torpedo or a mine.

When in 1943 I was a patient in Bristol at the Frenchay Hospital there were several local people who were convinced that Kitchener's death did not occur in the way it was officially announced. One man gave me many details of how the Germans transferred the famous Secretary of State for War at the height of the hurricane from the sinking *Hampshire* to the U-boat which carried him to Germany.

There are stories that Lord Kitchener met his death as the result of a World War I type Guy Fawkes plot, maneuvered by several members of the British cabinet. Many in London accused members of the cabinet of allowing Germany to know Kitchener was at sea on the way to Russia.

Unfortunately some of his colleagues in the cabinet did believe that Kitchener had outstayed his usefulness. They had ammunition for their beliefs in the unfortunate results of Mesopotamia and Gallipoli.

Another story is told that while Kitchener was in the Mediterranean the daughter of a leading member of the cabinet was married at St. Margaret's, Westminster. Almost every one of importance was present at the wedding, and with the Secretary of State for War in the Mediterranean, they acted "like schoolboys on a holiday." Just before the ceremony began, Lord Kitchener, who had unexpectedly returned from the East, walked up the aisle, and the countenances of his associates changed from happiness to dismay.

Indeed, it is possible that the Germans knew of Lord Kitchener's trip on the high seas to Russia. It is believed that there were men at Petrograd in the pay of the German government, as now we know there was widespread corruption all over Russia.

Actually Lord Horatio Kitchener's death was known in Copenhagen several hours before the news was released in London. We can still read in the back issues of a German periodical that Kitchener's obituary notice was taken from the morgue library the moment that his decision to journey to Russia was announced.

Lord Jellicoe spent many hours of his later life explaining why the *Hampshire*'s course was changed, as if to attempt to prove that he was not responsible for what happened.

Admiral von Scheer actually gives us the name of the officer aboard a U-boat which had laid mines in the area, Lieutenant Commander Kurt Beitzen, but, of course, this merely indicates that mines were in the vicinity. The admiral does not state one way or another if the mines were laid specifically to catch Lord Kitchener, and the official attitude of the British Admiralty is that the mine was laid "by the German submarine U-75 as part of Admiral Scheer's preliminary dispositions prior to the battle of Jutland."

Lord Jellicoe comments as follows: "I have often wondered since that fatal day, whether anything could have been done that was not done, but short of postponing the departure of the *Hampshire* altogether, . . . no safeguards were possible."

All official statements concur in the belief that Kitchener's death was the normal drowning in the ocean of a man aboard a sinking ship. Nevertheless, I must offer the thought that there are so many unsolved and unexplained fragments of this unusual story that the fate of Lord Kitchener must always remain a mystery.

CHAPTER 18

Sargasso Sea

I have never forgotten the stories my mother, Alice, told me of her experiences while sailing with her mother and father aboard the bark *Russell* in the Sargasso Sea, that mysterious area of ocean between Africa and America, where the bark was becalmed and entrapped for a relatively brief period during the year 1883.

After telling me of the strange 2,000,000 square mile area which has so many legends attached to it, she showed me the paintings of the Sargasso she had made almost eighty years ago and let me examine the curios she had taken from the sea at the time. She told me how she and her father rowed away one day from their becalmed bark. Alice picked up several fragments of the yellow seaweed and put a few of the tiny crabs with their queer paddle-shaped hind legs into a container. Later she glued her prizes onto a white sheet of paper. We still have these souvenirs of eighty years ago.

I have read much controversial material about the famous

Sargasso Sea, and without question there are scores of unsolved mysteries connected with it. The word Sargasso comes from the Portuguese, *Salgazo,* derived from a word which stands for tiny grapes, as much of the seaweed in the area has grape-shaped globes in the seaweed itself.

Since the beginning of the conquest of the Atlantic the Sargasso Sea is said to have drawn into its fatal calmness hundreds of vessels of all types. It has been asserted that many craft which have happened into its grasp float on for years, safe from almost every outside influence, drifting along to eternity under strange and obscure conditions.

Frankly, I doubt that all the stories I have heard of the Sargasso Sea are true. However, merely because scientists today can prove that the sea is free of floating hulks I do not think that they can announce with certainty this same condition was true a century ago. There is always something to be said on both sides of a question of this character.

This great seaweed area is located between 20° and 35° north latitude and 30° and 70° west longitude. The weed is not continuous, but exists only in patches. The size of the patches varies, controlled in part by wind and currents. In some places the seaweed is thin, floating only on the surface, while in others it extends far below the surface of the water.

Crawling over the surface of the Sargasso are all kinds of queer and revolting-looking fish. As late as the turn of the century the decaying hulls of ships, mostly derelicts, were reported from time to time.

A description by one who was imprisoned in the Sargasso Sea follows. It was found in the effects of Francis F. Haskell of Haverhill, Massachusetts, after his death several years ago:

It was 8 o'clock one evening, we had been drifting all day, when I got out of my bunk and ascended the companion ladder, to take charge of the first night watch. I had noticed a queer smell, like something very rank and rotten, directly I put my head outside my cabin door, and the higher I mounted the worse it grew, until by the time I had reached the deck, it was well-nigh unbearable, and when I looked around, I saw at once what caused it. About half a point away from us to starboard, was something that absolutely staggered me, it was so vast, and queer, and altogether unlike anything I had ever seen before. It was nothing more or less than a great greenish yellow desert, that stretched right away to the horizon, and arising from it, at intervals, in all directions, were the masts and funnels of countless ships, ships of all sizes, brigs, schooners, three-deckers, steamers, a regular hotchpotch of every conceivable build and age, but all absolutely motionless, with no sign of any life whatever on board them. They looked, indeed, so grim and dark and ghostly in the waning daylight, that I felt properly scared.

How that evening comes back to me! Away on the horizon the crimson sunset had paled into the most delicate pink and gold, which gradually merged into blue, the deepest and most wonderful blue I had ever seen. But beautiful as it was, it was the horror beneath, that great expanse of rank, rotten, yellow weed that fascinated me most. I simply could not take my eyes from it, but stood there, close beside Jim, watching and watching. And all the while the moon rose higher and higher in the heavens, bathing the silent, reeking mass in its cold white beams.

Another writer, quoted by Elliott O'Donnell in his *Boys' Book of Sea Mysteries,* tells of a Scot who was curious to see the notorious Sargasso. When he was passing along its western extremity he had a strange experience. He said:

The day was stiflingly hot, not a breath of wind, not a ripple on the water, which was like glass. I was leaning over the bulwarks, gazing at the vast expanse of yellow, motionless weed before me, when a strange thing happened. Right in front of me, coming out of the water, surrounded on all sides by weed, was a derelict three-master in advanced state of decay and dissolution. There were patches of green slimy looking stuff on its sides and a quantity of weed hanging to its figurehead and stern. A more dismal looking object it would have been difficult to imagine. It was absolutely motionless, and looked as if it had been there for ages. Suddenly, as I was staring at it, it rose a foot or two right above the surface of the weed, and then, falling down, sank through the weed, out of sight. It was gone in a trice.

"Well," I ejaculated to one of the crew who was standing near me, "what could have caused that—a squid?"

"I dunno, sir," the man replied, "I saw something rise up with the ship, but what it was I couldn't say; I've 'eard tell that there be all manner of strange creatures in that green stuff."

Much impressed and not a little awed by what he had seen, my informant gave orders to move away from the Sargasso at once, and the seaweed meadows were soon a mere speck in the distance.

The Sargasso Sea played an important part in the discovery of America. When the crews of Columbus were about to mutiny, the sea with its comforting daily sight of drifting vegetation played a very vital role. We are told that the sailors were astonished when they saw it, "in a manner, covered with green and yellow weeds, which seemed to have been lately washed away from some rock or island. This phenomenon gave them reason to conclude that they were near some land, especially when they perceived a live crab floating among the weeds." And a week later, on September 23, 1492, they saw "a tropic bird and such a quantity of weeds as alarmed the crew who began to fear that their course would be impeded." From September 16 until October 14, Columbus was in the Sargasso Sea.

Columbus' historian stated that the "air was Soft and Refreshing, and the Admiral says Nothing was Wanting but the Singing of the Nightingale; The Sea Smooth as a River. Many Weeds Appeared." They saw "Vast Schools of Tunnyfish, and the People on the *Nina* Killed one. The Admiral says that those Indications Came from the West, 'Where, I Hope in the Exalted God in Whose Hands are all Victories, That Land Will Very Soon Appear.'"

"At Dawn They Saw Many More Weeds, Apparently River Weeds, and Among Them a Live Crab, Which the Admiral Kept."

After his first voyage to the Western Hemisphere, Columbus warned the world of the Sargasso Sea:

When I came a hundred leagues west of the Azores, I noticed an extraordinary change in the aspect of the sky and the stars, in the temperature of the air and in that of the sea. I found the surface of the water covered so thickly with vegetation resembling small branches of fir that we believed we must be in shallow waters and that the ships would soon be aground for lack of depth.

The words of Columbus inspired terror of the Sargasso Sea in the minds of many seamen. Tormented by the fear of their vessels' being caught in the terrible sea, they feared that they would be becalmed for months.

In addition to truthful tales of trouble in the Sargasso, the sea came to form the subject of many a quarter-deck tale designed to curdle the blood of cabin boys. Not only were ships seized in the embraces of gigantic octopus-like weeds, but steamers and sailing vessels were overwhelmed by monstrous seaweed growths and their crews paralyzed by the breathless air, until they died of hunger. Frankly, I am at a loss to decide where the truth ends and the fiction begins.

The Sargasso has been the subject of many writers. One book told the story of a liner, the *Queen*, colliding with a derelict. Waterlogged, she drifted into the Sargasso Sea. The survivors discovered with surprise a community of castaways, led by a sea captain, living aboard the wrecks. There was even a chaplain available for marriages and funerals. Old-fashioned Spanish and Dutch craft with round bottoms, galleons loaded with gold, frigates battered by cannon balls, and even steamers of the 1850s were present.

A gruesome discovery was made on the edge of the Sargasso Sea in July, 1884, when the *Brittania*, bound for London from Buenos Aires, came across a sailing craft which had been abandoned. Many dead people were found aboard, but the vessel was never identified.

Then there is the "Little Sargasso." Few have heard of the Little Sargasso compared to the tens of millions who know of the Sargasso itself. Captain Walter E. Scott of Bucksport, Maine has preserved a tale of the Little Sargasso. This story, "forgotten by the past generation and unknown to the present, is an interesting historic record of the history of sailing ships," the famous captain tells us.

Captain Scott believes today as he always has, that both Sargasso Seas hold the answer to many of our unsolved mysteries. His story of the Little Sargasso is about the Italian bark *Herat* which put in at Bridgetown, Barbados, in February, 1913, after one of the strangest and most mysterious passages in marine history. Although she had not traveled far, as the gull flies, she had yet sailed thousands of miles.

The *Herat,* rated at Lloyd's as a proper 100 1A bark, was of 1,394 tons net register. She left Gulfport, Mississippi, on July 19, 1912, for Buenos Aires. Her sailing route took her out over the gulf through the Yucatan channel, between Cape Catouche and Cape San Antonio, and across the Caribbean to the southward of the Windward Islands, and so on down the great highway for sailing craft to the mouth of the Plate, some 7,000 miles away.

On her last trip south she had made the passage from New York to Argentina in only seventy-eight days, and there was no reason to believe she would take longer on her present journey. Her master, Captain Bertolotto, had planned to make better time than on his previous trip, for Gulfport, Mississippi, is not as far from the Plate as is New York.

When several months had gone by without any word of the *Herat,* her agents practically gave her up for lost. Then, many months after she sailed away the agents in New York were surprised to receive a cable that she had reported at Barbados for a fresh supply of stores. All her provisions had become exhausted and her crew had been put on short rations.

Where had she been? What had she been doing all this time? The answers were never given to the satisfaction of the average sailor, but I have been able to piece together many of the obscure fragments of the puzzle.

Only once after leaving Gulfport had the *Herat* been reported. That was in July in the Gulf of Mexico. Some hundreds of miles out from the port of his departure Captain Bertolotto, having passed the 100-fathom curve, encountered a westerly blow, which bore him, after a long delay, to a rarely traversed part of the Gulf of Mexico. Directly to the northward of the Yucatan channel, between Cuba and Yucatan, it is known as the Little Sargasso Sea.

After another terrific blow, which, however, was of short duration, the skipper found himself with fore upper topsails razored by the gale into whiplashes, the vessel drifting within the area of a sudden and unexpected calm—a sea within a sea —an astonishing expanse of dead water.

Outside this calmness the waves were great, rolling breakers, resembling the froth on a boiling kettle, but inside the area the lumber-laden vessel was part of a floating city, abounding in driftwood, weeds, trunks of trees, overturned half-wrecked boats, logs from Yucatan, orange trees from Florida, and ribs of wrecked ships with clinging barnacles. Most astonishing of all was a derelict schooner, barely showing her jibboomless bowsprit above the greasy water. Her heavier stern, submerged, dragged below the afterpart of the slimy hull, which was encrusted with shells and green with sea growth. The derelict, protruding its snout like a turtle from the lifeless water, had been so long a creature of the currents that all traces of her name and hailing port were obliterated.

Sea birds hovered around the awesome "backyard" of the ocean, while water serpents sunned themselves upon the low-

lying corners of ancient wreckage or slipped splashing grue-
somely into the almost hidden waters.

The Italian seamen aboard the *Herat* crossed themselves
in their terror, for never had they beheld sights so weird and
awesome. The *Herat* now began a remarkable circling. Dead
flat calms developed which were the direct opposite of the
violent seas that had driven the vessel into the quiet spot.
Two branches of the Gulf Stream, flowing in opposite directions at that season of the year in which the *Herat* had been
traveling, began to dominate the "dead sea" in such a fashion that the vessel was caught as it were inside a double whirlpool.

The bark was in the Little Sargasso Sea, known as the
"Central Sea," temporarily in its semiyearly existence but
nevertheless a scientific reality. In August, 1912, the "Central
Sea" existed longer than ordinarily, with dead calms in the
center which outside winds and waves could not break.

The water in which the ship was now caught was of a greenish, muddy tint, greatly discolored and cold. It seemed as
though the waters of the Mississippi, while passing across the
Gulf, had been collected and held imprisoned in the circular
sea by its enforced rotary movement. From it, for a score of
days, there was no escape for the imprisoned ship. The two
opposing branches of the Gulf Stream clutched the *Herat* between them night and day. The northwest branch flowed
from Yucatan channel across the Gulf almost to the delta of
the Mississippi where it mingled with the main Gulf Stream,
and in this stronger current flowed to the southwest and so
on, out through the Straits of Florida to the sea.

Finally meteorological events shaped themselves to liberate
the *Herat* from her horrible circular, aimless voyaging, dur-

ing which her crew could do naught but tease the lifeless airs above by hauling the mainyards around, constantly pulling on braces, and whistle, pray, and swear. The *Herat* began to accumulate heavy marine growth and barnacles.

During the captain's plight, in which he would have welcomed the worst hurricane that the stormy Gulf could produce, it was maddening to study the effect of the waters of the Mississippi upon the natural seas. The river water appeared to act like oil in smoothing down the sea.

In their enforced imprisonment simulating the *Flying Dutchman's* endless voyage, the crew became almost insane, feeling that something had cursed and doomed them forever to sail round and round. Fifty sunrises and fifty sunsets had come and gone since they left port, and they should by that time have been off Cape San Roque.

On the morning of the twenty-first day in the enchanted circle, there came evidences of a fearful norther, the darkening effects of which could be seen beyond the mile stretch between the inner circling and the outer rim of the "dead center."

When the storm hit, it broke over the inner "Central Sea," sending along the living derelict with a swifter motion. The effect was like that of an army breaking ranks, for muddy water, debris, wreckage, and vegetation began to travel suddenly eastward, making a fearful commotion and an unopposed exit from the inner sea. The *Herat* was caught in the mighty eastward movement, and before the skipper, almost mad from the uncanniness of his position, could get stripped down to fore lower topsails and one jib, he was bowled along, free of the whirlpool, toward the inner Florida coast by the combined effect of the norther and the swirling current.

By porting his helm and swinging his yards around, hauling in his forebraces, he headed to the southward before it was too late. He had intended to take the Cape San Roque track, but another great hurricane blew him so far to the northwest and beyond the limit of the northeast trades that in disgust he returned to Barbados, a port he had left during the previous year on May 16. On a former trip he had consumed only 22 days in making Gulfport, whereas now he had taken 104 days to sail and waste the same distance from Gulfport to Barbados, in the meanwhile reducing the crew to a fast and then a famine.

The Sargasso Sea should interest the gourmet, as it is the birthplace of eels. Both American and European eels swim the hundreds upon hundreds of miles to breed there, but the two varieties never intermix. The young eels, transparent as glass, then start back to the same fresh-water streams and pools where their mothers and fathers spent most of their lives.

By the time the European larvae reach home, usually a three-year period, they have become elvers, or young eels. The American eels take only one year, as the distance is much less. The parent eels, their purpose in existence evidently at an end, sink slowly to the bottom of the Sargasso and die.

Also in the Sargasso Sea are unbelievable varieties of other fish, snails, octopuses, crabs, and shrimp. The sargassum fish is so unusually strange that a member of one of the expeditions to the Sargasso exclaimed "My Word!" when he first saw it. The fish is now called by the same name, My Word. Its real title is *Histrio histrio,* or *pterophryne.* Looking exactly like the seaweed through which it swims, the small six-inch creature can stalk its prey unnoticed. Then, with a gulp of its oversize mouth, it can swallow whole its unsuspecting victim.*

The visit of Charles William Beebe added much of importance to the average man's knowledge of the Sargasso Sea. When Beebe visited there on the *Arcturus* in the year 1925 he captured two eels in his net. One of them had been destined to complete its growth in faraway Lake Ontario and the other in a little stream near the headwaters of the Rhine River, according to Beebe.†

As the majority of deep-sea animals are small, the sailors on the *Arcturus* seldom lacked comedy. On one occasion when there was a shout of "Whales astern!" and every door erupted flying figures that raced aft, the oldest able seaman, a big, bored Scandinavian was heard to mutter, "I seen plenty whales. I never seen such funny folks."

Hundreds of specimens had to be examined as fast as possible, Mr. Beebe tells us, and "soon every desk in the laboratory had an absorbed worker armed with forceps, spoons and pipettes, disentangling fish from sagittae, crustaceans from jellyfish, squids from siphonophores." The delicate mass that is scrambled together by a trailing net is so fragile that it seems a "miracle to float out a double handful in a dish of water and find that most of the animals are not damaged." Mr. Beebe considered it incredible that the contact with the net and the water impact on the upward journey should not crush all but the largest and toughest.

One day, in the dark-room of the *Arcturus,* Mr. Beebe shouted out: "Astronesthes and Oneirodes!"

---

* The My Word fish will eat anything, even another My Word fish. Marine biologists suggest that the My Word cannibals call a truce at the appropriate time, or they would soon be extinct.

† Charles William Beebe, *The Arcturus Adventure,* p. 24.

This was not an ancient Grecian oath, as Mr. Beebe explained, but the names of two luminous deep-sea fish that were gratifying the hope with which they had been hurried into the darkroom. Brought up from a region where the pressure on their small bodies was hundreds of pounds to the square inch, into an unfamiliar zone where it amounted to only fifteen pounds, it was marvelous that they lived to reach the surface. They continued to exist long enough to show little lights which up to the moment of capture had been gliding about in the blackness of the great depths.

Both of these particular ones had a velvety black skin. Astronesthes was rather slim and long-bodied, with a slender tentacle trailing from its chin, which, to Beebe's surprise, was delicately luminous down its entire length, only the thickened tip showing no light. This very fish was later captured at the surface at night. Oneirodes was a globular fish, chiefly mouth. It sprouted an appendage from the top of its head. From the end of the appendage dangled a tiny light, for all the world like an electric bulb. This hung before the fish as it swam along and attracted the smaller creatures upon which it fed.

Mr. Beebe's expedition on the *Arcturus* sailed from Brooklyn on February 11, 1925, and returned to New York on July 30 of the same year.

On a pleasant day in the year 1869 there was launched from the Camden, Maine, shipyard a beautiful bark which was christened the *J. G. Norwood.** For more than a score

---

* Her measurements were length 121 feet, breadth 31 feet and depth 16 feet. Her tonnage was 418.89, and her official number was 75148. Her signal letters were J. G. V. Q.

and a half of years she sailed the high seas without attracting unusual attention. One day when the loading of her cargo of cotton was completed at Galveston, Texas, she sailed for Europe carrying aboard an orphaned cabin boy named Elisha Thompson.

When three weeks out on her journey, she ran into a terrible storm, and the next morning the captain and six others were swept overboard when a gigantic wave of green water swept right across the stern. Only three were left on the *Norwood*, and of these, two were killed by the mainmast when it fell, leaving Elisha alone on the bark. The *Norwood* drifted for the next four weks, until Elisha realized the vessel had reached the edge of the Sargasso Sea.

On the first day after his arrival there, Elisha took stock of the situation. The splintered stump of the foremast was all that remained. The port tail had been pulled into the sea for twenty feet where the mast had crashed down through it. The mizzenmast lay across the skylight of the cabin. Although the main topmast had fallen, the mainmast itself was still standing.

Two of the boats remained, but were splintered and smashed, and all the other boats were missing. The *Norwood* lay with her stern high in the air, but her bow was so deep in the water that the sea came up to the base of the mainmast.

As far as Elisha could see, the ocean was full of seaweed, in which floated a variety of flotsam and wreckage, ship's timbers, and fragments of masts. In the distance was the wreck of a steamer, floating on an even keel, and beyond it the hulk of a wooden ship, waterlogged. In back of the two craft was such a confusion of wrecks that Elisha could not make out where one began and another left off.

The next day the *Norwood* had worked her way into solid wreckage, and Elisha decided to explore the mass of wrecked ships. He was up early, making a small lunch so that he would not have to return until dark. There was enough food in the galley to last one man several years.

Elisha started out across first one craft and then another until he reached the *City of Boston,* a great iron steamer. A short distance away was what he finally decided was an eighteen-gun sloop-of-war. Entering the cabin, he found that he was aboard the long-missing American sloop-of-war *Wasp,* and copied several of the items in the log:

9:52   Our main-mast by the board and our mizzen badly wounded. Action again severe. Few of our men left.

9:56   Captain Blakeley killed and brought below.

10:15   The enemy sinking. We cannot help him. Most of our men are dead. All of us living are badly hurt.

The last entry, quoted above as of 10:15, indicated that all aboard were mortally wounded and would die. Evidently, after the battle, the *Wasp* drifted helplessly into the Sargasso Sea.

Later Elisha worked his way across several other craft to reach what he realized was a Spanish galleon, and he went aboard. In the hold there was a fortune in gold, but it was worthless to Elisha.

Many months went by before Thompson hit upon a plan to escape. He had soon grown weary of living in that strange community of abandoned derelicts inhabited by scores of skeletons, and decided to reach a craft from which he could take a lifeboat and sail away.

Finally he obtained a compass from the binnacle of a derelict schooner and located a lifeboat which had a small sail. It was the work of a week to stock the lifeboat with a liberal supply of drinking water, wine, and ship biscuit. On one fine morning he set sail, or rather began drifting away from the Sargasso Sea.

Two days later a light breeze sprang up, and five days after that he sighted his first vessel far in the distance. Two days following that he came up on the vessel, but to his horror he found it was just another derelict.

Ten days went by before a second craft was sighted. This time it was a steamer, and those on the ship noticed Elisha's lifeboat. The steamer changed her course, and he was hauled aboard an hour later.

He told his adventures, but, of course, no one believed him, especially the part about the gold on the Spanish galleon. Reaching Liverpool, England, the captain of the rescue craft took Elisha ashore, where the boy wrote out the entire history of what had happened. Although he had been in fair health on the voyage to Liverpool, he suddenly became ill and died, leaving his notes as the only evidence of as strange an experience as can be imagined.

CHAPTER 19

Mount Blanc and *Mount Hood*

There have been many great explosions in the history of the United States and Canada, and the one which occurred in Halifax harbor is well known to many of this generation. On the morning of December 6, 1917, two ships, the *Mount Blanc* and the *Imo,* collided in Halifax Harbor, causing what forever afterward has been called the Halifax Disaster.

Back at New York, the *Mount Blanc,* a French ammunition craft which had put aboard a deadly cargo of picric acid, benzol, and trinitrotoluene, was on her way to Bedford Basin for convoy. The Norwegian ship *Imo* was loaded with goods for Belgian relief, as a huge sign in red letters on a white background stated. She was outbound.

For some strange, forever to be unknown, reason, the two craft came together, with the *Imo* knifing deep into the vitals of the ammunition ship, spilling the benzol against the rest of the cargo. The benzol poured into the picric acid, setting it afire, and soon the great *Mount Blanc* was ablaze.

Ordering full speed astern, the captain of the *Imo* slowly backed her toward the Dartmouth shore. Aboard the *Mount Blanc* the forty-two members of the ship's company launched two lifeboats, rowed desperately for the opposite shore, landed on the beach, and disappeared almost at once into the dense woods there. They knew what lay ahead!

Alone, but noticed by hundreds along the shore, the blazing *Mount Blanc* drifted down the harbor toward the open sea. All over the city the day was barely beginning for the people of Halifax. Workmen were already engaged at their duties in the various factories along the water front, while businessmen were on their journeys to their offices. The housewives had just sent the children off for school and were getting ready to do their shopping.

Then, cutting through the early morning noises came the terrifying sound of the fire alarm, for a watcher had sighted the burning ship and notified the fire department. Many workers looked out into the harbor at the *Mount Blanc*. They were frightened but fascinated as they watched the beautiful blue-green flames leaping higher and higher in the air, changing to great billows of grayish smoke far overhead.

Suddenly, as they watched spellbound, there was a terrific, cataclysmic concussion, followed a split-second later by a detonation which overwhelmed everything. The *Mount Blanc* had exploded!

A tidal wave roared toward shore, swept up over the water front, and then receded almost as fast as it had formed. Tugs, schooners, and ships all thumped on the harbor bottom as the wave rushed back into the bay. The *Imo*, battered ashore by the wave, was pushed high on the beach at Dartmouth. The explosion itself had literally wiped out every home, office building, church, school, and factory along the waterfront, leaving only rubble and rubbish in their places.

A battered hulk, what remained of the *Mount Blanc,* could be seen protruding from the harbor water. The Halifax Narrows will always be associated with this terrible disaster, for almost 2,000 people were killed there, and 6,000 others were injured. Ten thousand persons were made homeless, and the total damage amounted to more than $35,000,000.*

On the morning of November 10, 1944, there occurred another great explosion which rivaled in intensity the Halifax disaster.

At that time the U.S.S. *Mount Hood* was anchored in Seeadler Harbor at Manus in the Admiralty Islands. On the day before, a Japanese plane had flown over the *Mount Hood* at a height so great that no one in the area realized the plane was there until the navy airstrip was sprayed with machine-gun bullets. No one was injured, and there was really no great damage.

Then, at three minutes past 8:00 A.M. on November 10 came the terrific convulsion caused by the instantaneous blast of 4,500 tons of explosives aboard the *Mount Hood.* At that moment Commander Chester A Gile was seven and a half miles from the *Mount Hood,* actually making an investigation concerning the nuisance air raid of November 9.

He stated, "I had gone up the harbor in my capacity as Base Intelligence Officer to the Aviation Supply Depot on Los Negros Island." Commander Gile's efforts were inter-

---

* On July 17, 1944, two munition ships blew up at Port Chicago, California, killing 322 persons. In 1945 an exploding naval arsenal rocked Halifax again, but the results were not comparable.

rupted "by a tremendous B-O-O-O-M! It sounded as though a single beat had been struck on a gigantic bass drum—a drum a mile in diameter. There was a violent shock. The ground quivered as though in an earthquake. Looking down harbor, I saw a pillar of blue-gray smoke expanding and rising to a height of a mile, against the cloudless sky."

As he and the others watched, three planes came in flying low over their heads from the direction of the explosion and headed out to sea. The planes were U. S. Navy types and bore American markings. "There was one bomber, with a fighter close on each wing. As the time between the blast and the appearance of the planes was about two minutes, just time enough for them to have been at the explosion and reach Los Negros, my first reaction was that they were captured planes manned by Japanese, and that they had bombed something in the harbor. I called on the photographer I had brought with me to photograph the planes. He snapped two quick exposures, which might have been very useful. But, in his excitement, he forgot to remove the cover from his lens. So no pictures!"

The ill-fated *Mount Hood* had been anchored in a direct line from land through the entrance of Seeadler Harbor. The possibility therefore existed that she might have been torpedoed by an enemy submarine outside the harbor, but all checks made at the harbor entrance indicated none had been there.

The control post on the island relayed the information that the lookout in the tower saw a burst of light flash upward from the *Mount Hood* "like lightning striking up." Calling the officer of the day, the lookout reported that he thought there was a ship on fire in the harbor. The officer asked him to repeat his statement. "I say I think there's a ship on fire in the harbor." Then a few seconds later came the terrific explosion.

Similar reports in World War I of ammunition ships which had blown up indicated that at both Halifax and Archangel each explosion was preceded several seconds by the same type of upward flash, and in those final seconds the ships appeared to be undamaged.

Unfortunately the *Mount Hood* had been anchored in the midst of a group of vessels which included all types of craft in the Seventh Fleet Service Force. Many lives would have been saved had the ammunition ship been anchored away from the others. It had been customary for the vessels carrying explosive cargoes to anchor immediately off the supply depot at Lugos, and someone had blundered in allowing the *Mount Hood* to be moored so near the other ships.

About two hundred craft were in the Seeadler Harbor on that November 10. There were transport ships, depot ships, tankers, cargo ships, destroyers, and destroyer escorts. Indeed it was fortunate that the explosion did not occur a month earlier when Seeadler Harbor was jammed with all types of vessels of the Seventh Fleet to the number of 995.

It has never been explained how the explosion took place. Four hours after the blast, came the noon broadcast from Tokyo announcing that the American craft had been blown up in Manus Harbor that morning. As Commander Gile brought out in his article in the *U. S. Naval Institute Proceedings, February 1963,* the expression "blown up" was used instead of "blew up" or "exploded," conveying the implication that the Japanese caused the disaster. The Japanese later, at six that night, repeated the story and added the list of the craft which had been damaged, including the *Mindanao,* which was riddled with flying fragments from the *Mount Hood.*

Nothing of the ship remained after the explosion except segments of metal which stuck to other craft. No human remains were ever discovered; no supplies of any sort, nothing made of wood or paper except a few pages of a signal notebook found floating on the water about one-half mile away. Also, many harbor craft vanished with all hands, and thirty others were peppered with flying fragments. The patrol-craft tender *Mindanao* was simply riddled from stem to stern as though she had been under heavy fire.

Total casualties were close to a thousand, and not one person of the 350 aboard the *Mount Hood* survived. Every officer and man aboard was killed instantly. The only survivors from the munitions ship were six men who left the ship a short time before the explosion. Two of them were prisoners being transferred to the base brig to await trial by court-martial, who were released at once because of the disaster. The other four composed a party who were at the base post office picking up mail for those aboard the *Mount Hood,* mail which would never be delivered. The survivors, under cross-examination revealed that in some instances there had been carelessness in the handling of explosives. On one occasion it was admitted a sling load of ammunition had struck against the side of a ship.

Every officer and enlisted man above deck was killed outright on the *Mindanao,* with eighty-two men below deck dying eventually from the explosion.

On November 12, natives living on the south side of Manus reported they had seen flashing green lights off the coast which some believed might have been a Japanese submarine signaling to coastwatchers. Commander Gile tells of a small island, Anabat, thirty miles southeast of Manus. It is about one mile in diameter and uninhabited. On November 17 when Commander Gile took a party there to investigate, he found "no evidence of enemy activity, but we did find something else. This was a bulletproof gasoline tank of 600 gallons capacity. Grass was still green under the tank, an indication that it had been lying there only a very brief time. Translation of name plates identified the tank as having been jettisoned from a Japanese four-engine bomber. No such bomber had previously been reported in the whole area, including Rabaul, and this particular bomber had not been detected at all. It was concluded that the tank had been dropped by the reconnaissance plane which had flown over Manus the day before the disaster."

A board of investigation was held aboard the U.S.S. *Sierra* immediately after the explosion. For one month the board gathered evidence and heard testimony. The findings indicated that no submarine could have attacked the *Mount Hood*, and the investigating board ruled out air attack as well. Neither was any possible connection indicated between the marked planes flying away from the scene and the explosions. Nothing could be decided, however, concerning the Japanese reconnaissance plane which had jettisoned the gas tank on Anabat Island.

Although the *Mount Hood* had been anchored in about 40 feet of water, the explosion blasted a trench in the harbor bottom 250 feet wide and 1,000 feet long, to a depth of 85 feet. Divers later found in this trench the largest remaining fragment of the ship's hull, the piece being just less than 100 feet long. Destruction was unbelievably complete.

As in many other mysteries of the sea, the enigma of the explosion aboard the *Mount Hood* probably will never be solved.

CHAPTER 20

Joyita

In my recent volume, *Women of the Sea*, I tell of a little girl, Terry Jo Duperrault, who was the sole survivor of a strange sea mystery of the Atlantic Ocean. Captain Julian Harvey, of the yacht *Bluebelle*, evidently murdered everyone aboard except Terry Jo. It is probable that he carried out this infamous act to obtain the insurance on his wife, after which he scuttled the ship and saved himself. When Terry Jo was later rescued at sea, Harvey committed suicide.

Insurance or family trouble of some sort may have been the reason for another earlier tragedy at sea, this time aboard the *Joyita*, which was found abandoned in the South Pacific several years before the *Bluebelle* incident.

On a pleasant October afternoon in 1955 a sturdy two-engine motor vessel sailed away from Apia in Western Samoa. Her destination was the Tokelau Islands 290 miles to the north. The *Joyita* was a routine ship, sixty-nine feet long and registered at seventy tons. One of her claims to fame was the fact that she had once served as Mary Pickford's personal pleasure yacht. Now she was just another vessel carrying passengers, oil, timber, and food supplies.

On board were a crew of five and twenty passengers, including two children. The captain was Thomas Henry "Dusty" Miller, a middle-aged Welshman who always wore a lava-lava * at sea. Captain Miller had an excellent reputation as an experienced, level-headed seaman, but he was known to be in some financial difficulty. Serving as Miller's mate was an American Indian, "Chuck" Simpson, who was making his last voyage before settling down on a Pacific island with his Samoan wife.

Due to arrive in the Tokelaus forty hours after leaving Apia, the *Joyita* did not reach her destination in her usual time. As the days went by and she remained missing, concern was felt by friends and relatives of those aboard. No violent storms had been reported, no distress signals were ever received, and nothing was found by the three planes that scoured more than one hundred thousand square miles of the Pacific. The *Joyita* had vanished completely, as scores of other ships have done since man first took to the sea.†

The *Joyita* did appear again, but under circumstances which brought scores of puzzling questions, most of which are still unanswered. Not since 1872, when the brigantine *Mary Celeste* was found under sail in the Atlantic with not a soul on board,** had there been a maritime riddle to equal the one posed by the finding of the *Joyita*. More than a month had passed after she had sailed, during which time there was

* Male sarong.

† An outstanding article on *Joyita* was written by Leslie Hobbs in *Life,* Dec. 12, 1955.

** See my *Mysterious Tales of the New England Coast,* pp. 114–133.

no word at all. Then, on November 10, thirty-eight days after the *Joyita* left Apia, a motor vessel named *Tuvalu* was passing the Fiji Islands. Ninety miles north of Vanua Levu the *Tuvalu* sighted a listing ship wallowing in a light sea. Drawing closer, the *Tuvalu*'s captain noticed a huge hole in the superstructure of the craft. On closer examination the vessel was identified as the missing *Joyita,* but she had strayed or drifted almost six hundred miles from her regular port-to-port track.

A boat was sent over to take a careful look, but no one boarded the *Joyita* at that time, and there was obviously no sign of life on the craft. After making certain that no living person was on the vessel, the captain radioed Fiji: "IT SOUNDS LIKE ANOTHER MARY CELESTE. WE HAVE NO THEORY YET WHAT HAPPENED."

Some time afterward another craft, the Fijian tender *Degei,* sighted the drifting derelict, and two ship's officers from her went aboard to attach a towline. Captain Robert James checked every part of the *Joyita* that was not underwater but found "no bodies, no lifeboats or rafts, no food in the galley or in any of the other compartments above water, no log, no sextant." *

The *Degei* towed the listing *Joyita* to the harbor of Vanua Levu, Fiji. An official investigation revealed that in spite of the hole in the superstructure and the pronounced list, the *Joyita* was still seaworthy even after more than a month in the Pacific.

The questions now began to be asked, as similar questions had been asked almost three-quarters of a century before concerning the *Mary Celeste* incident. What had happened to the

* *Life* Magazine, Dec. 12, 1955.

twenty-five persons on the *Joyita,* and why had they deserted an apparently sound ship? No one has yet provided satisfactory answers.

At Vanua Levu, a port with limited facilities, workmen went aboard the *Joyita* and pumped the water out. Then the craft was towed to the Fijian port of Suva, where it was hauled up on a slip for inspection. Engineering and salvage experts were soon engaged to discover what had happened.

When the experts went aboard the *Joyita* they met an unpleasant odor of decay. This was only to be expected, as the craft had been partly submerged for a long time. The investigators found a mess of soggy wreckage littering the cabin and the engine room, but they were quick to announce that the *Joyita* was still fundamentally sound. Barnacles growing above the regular waterline proved that the *Joyita* had been listing steeply for several weeks, but it was agreed that the hull's damage was caused by breaking waves smashing against the craft.

As in the case several years later aboard the *Bluebelle,* disaster had overtaken the ship at night. The light switches and the masthead navigation light were in the "on" position, and the ship's clock had stopped at 10:53. There were indications of engine failure, with one engine covered by a mattress, and the other showing that repairs had been attempted.

A deck awning was evidence that some of the passengers had been sleeping outside on the night of the trouble. Two possible reasons for sleeping there were the steamy tropical heat or the lack of enough bunks for the ship's company. All the lifesaving equipment was missing. It consisted of a sixteen-foot boat with an outboard motor, a sixteen-man life raft, and two ten-man life rafts. The two compasses and two radio sets had disappeared, together with almost every other movable object that might have been useful on the open sea. Food which normally would be stored in the galley was missing, but the refrigerators contained a substantial supply of meat, which under ordinary conditions would be taken by people abandoning a craft at sea and going aboard a lifeboat or raft. Saloon furniture was missing, but, of course, it might have been thrown overboard. All indications were that the twenty-five men, women, and children evidently had a limited amount of time in which to make their escape.

Was the disaster which occurred that October night between Apia and Tokelau known only to the twenty-five people aboard, or did others overcome them?

A possibility that the *Joyita* was struck by a waterspout has been suggested. Many ships have been hit by this marine phenomenon, but even if a waterspout had smashed into the ship, the group which had abandoned her must have believed that she would soon sink. They would have attempted to return to the *Joyita* later rather than stay in boats and rafts at sea. Leslie Hobbs suggests that "darkness might have prevented them finding the *Joyita* again and they possibly lost their lives attempting to reach land in their small boat." *

A short time later the theory was put forward that the *John Williams VI,* the London missionary schooner, might have been in the same general area as the *Joyita.* Several of the crew, it was stated, had noticed seven waterspouts. Actually, when the theory was investigated, not only had the *Williams* not been in the area at the same time that the *Joyita* was supposed to have been there, but even when she did sail through

* *Life,* Dec. 12, 1955.

the same vicinity no one aboard had sighted even one single waterspout.

Leslie Hobbs in *Life* discusses the possibility that pirates took over the *Joyita*. The *Fiji Times and Herald* quoted "irreproachable" sources disclosing that search planes had photographed the Japanese fishing fleet lying directly across the *Joyita*'s course. Possibly one Japanese craft had piratically minded men aboard. It was suggested that the pirates attempted to blow up the ship and had then opened a seacock. On investigation no seacock was found open. Shortly afterward the British colonial office issued a statement from Mr. A. F. R. Stoddart, Fiji's colonial secretary, announcing that the report of the fishing fleet photograph was not true. Japanese shipowners, aroused by the piracy claim, called the story preposterous and insulting.

However, it is true that *Joyita* passenger A. K. Williams was carrying the equivalent of almost $3,000 in cash, and Captain Miller also had a sum approaching that amount. In his article Leslie Hobbs dismisses the piracy theory by stating that few people believe that "even larger sums of money than those mentioned would tempt criminals to piracy in this day and age." In this I do not agree, as I have studied far too many examples of murder carried out for much smaller sums of money, far less than the thousands which were aboard the *Joyita*.

Then, of course, the engines may have failed in bad weather, as we know that one of the engines was being repaired at the time.

There are those who are certain that the *Joyita* was run down by another craft. Although no sea captain of the area has come forward with the report of a collision, it may have taken place. In the case of Captain Joshua Slocum,* who was run down at sea near one of the Lesser Antilles, the truth of the matter was not revealed for years.

Many people believe that someone in the crew had planned to scuttle the *Joyita*. Nevertheless, scuttling a craft of this size with the elimination of at least twenty-four people would be quite a proposition, substantial enough to have tested the ability of another Captain Julian Harvey of the *Bluebelle*.

Another fact which must be taken into consideration is that some time before hearing of the disaster, in Cardiff, Wales, Beatrice Mathilda Miller began divorce proceedings against her husband, Captain "Dusty" Miller, of the *Joyita*. When the *Joyita* was listed as overdue, Mrs. Miller's counsel asked for a postponement of the hearing, later requesting an adjournment. Did Captain Miller disappear in this convenient manner to avoid paying alimony? This is almost too ridiculous to consider, but stranger things have happened.

Some additional basic known facts should be mentioned. The motor vessel *Joyita* was built in 1931 at the Wilmington Boat Works in Los Angeles. In 1950 she was sold to William Tavares of Honolulu. In September, 1952, Dr. Ellen Katherine Luomala, from Finland, an anthropologist and lecturer at the University of Hawaii, purchased the *Joyita*. Dr. Luomala actually bought the craft for Dusty Miller, a former lieutenant commander in the British naval forces. Dusty and Miss Luomala had fallen in love and were planning to marry when the divorce came through from his wife.

On Saturday, October 1, 1955, Dusty Miller had loaded the *Joyita* with sugar, rice, fuel oil, lumber, flour, and the usual trading goods. Mr. Pearless, the district officer for the Toke-

* See my *Mysterious Tales of the New England Coast*, p. 183.

laus, A. D. Parsons of Apia Hospital, J. Hodgkinson of Apia Hospital, and six Tokelau Islanders were included in the passenger list.

Chuck Simpson, the engineer, was an American Indian. It is believed that J. Wallwork and G. K. Williams were the only Europeans aboard. The remainder of the ship's company were Tokelaus and Gilbert Islanders.

Very little more has been found about the *Joyita* in the intervening years except the cause of her trouble. A one-inch cooling system water pipe of the port auxiliary engine had broken, allowing sea water to enter the hull at a rate of 1,700 gallons an hour. Nevertheless, the *Joyita* probably could have floated for years, because she was a very buoyant vessel. Heavily planked, she was insulated in all three holds with five-inch slabs of cork and had a number of empty oil drums in the hold.

There have been many conjectures, so many, in fact, that they approach in number those made about what happened to the people aboard the *Mary Celeste* almost ninety years before. But until June, 1958, all conjectures were without basis.

Then, early in June, 1958, the skeletons of six humans were found in a cave on uninhabited Henderson Island, located about a hundred miles from Pitcairn, where the *Bounty* mutineers under Fletcher Christian landed in the eighteenth century. Apparently the skeletons were of relatively recent date, and the possibility that they might be from the *Joyita* was seriously considered. The officials at Pitcairn requested that the six skeletons be placed in airtight coffins and transported to London or New Zealand for examination and possible identification. This request was turned down by the British authorities.

A short time later a fragment of hair from one of the skeletons was inspected pathologically in Suva, Fiji. The results were inconclusive, but it is still believed by some that at least six of those aboard the *Joyita* were captured and taken to Henderson Island where they were marooned and where they died of an unknown illness in the cave.

I have asked the governor general of Pitcairn Island if he could send the skull of one of the skeletons to Harvard University in Cambridge, Massachusetts, where anthropologist Edward Hunt has agreed to make an examination as to possible date of death and age of victim.

Although Dr. Hunt admits that there is a possibility that the remains are from the shipwreck in question, he is of the opinion that it is more probable that the skeletons found are from a Polynesian family whose members may have died under normal conditions.

Dr. Hunt explained that in many cases in the southern Pacific caves were used for the deposit of the native dead. The religious observances were an established part of the life of these islanders, and the caves were often used as the final resting places of those who were outstandingly religious.

I look with interest to a letter of reply from the governor general of Pitcairn Island, which may decide this particular question of whether or not the six bodies may be from the *Joyita*'s crew or passengers.

CHAPTER 21

Pamir

The German sailing ship *Pamir,* which was closely associated with the great commercial house established by Ferdinand Laeisz, is now at the bottom of the sea. In the last few years of her existence this steel four-masted bark made headlines whenever she arrived in port or sailed away, as she was a commercial, deep-water, wind-propelled vessel, one of the few survivors of her rig afloat.

To many who followed the sea either as a profession or as a hobby, a mention of the *Pamir* was always of interest. Her departures from and arrivals in European and South American ports would reawaken memories of the days of old, bringing back names such as Robert Hilgendord and Reederei F. Laeisz.

The long, glorious history of the Laeisz sailing ships of Hamburg, Germany, is not as well known as it should be. For those of us concerned only with clipper ship days, the great German sailing vessels, many of them using the letter "P" in their name, made records which may never be broken. The motto of the "Flying P" was, as Laeisz stated, "My ships can and will make rapid voyages."

Indeed it was a dramatic sight when a Laeisz ship would sail into a crowded anchorage. Shortening sail on the way in, seamen would also be rigging cargo gear and opening hatches to get ready for a quick handling of the cargo even before the anchor rattled down. The departure of a Laeisz ship also was accomplished with similar speed and economy of motion, and will never be forgotten.

Along with such craft as the *Preussen,* the *Potosi,* the *Padua,* and the *Passat,* the *Pamir* was beloved by millions who followed the sea. The 3,150-ton four-master was a solid craft. Built in 1905 at the Bloehm and Voss yards in Hamburg, she apparently was destined to live forever. During her half-century on the high seas, she had survived World War I without trouble and had weathered many gales.

Obtained by the Italian government in 1924, the *Pamir* was sold to Gustav Erickson of Finland, owner of a large fleet of sailing ships. He would not have bought her, together with her sister ship the *Passat,* unless he considered her outstandingly seaworthy. Both these reliable sailing cargo ships were put in service on the Australian run. They brought wheat and other goods to Europe, earning good money during an eight-year period.

The *Pamir* fell into British hands when World War II began. Impounded and registered in the New Zealand navy, she served for a time as a school ship. During the war the bark made six journeys to the west coast of America. A British grain importer chartered her for four years, putting her in the Australian corn cargo business. Then, although there was an acute shortage of merchant shipping at the time, the British company gave the *Pamir* back to Erickson.

A Belgian salvage company bought the *Pamir* and the *Passat,* outbidding the shipbreakers. Meanwhile, in Western Germany, groups insisted that the two ships should be acquired for training German marine officers. The reason for this demand was that a first-class German marine officer, in order to qualify for a position, had to have sailed as a boy in one of the big windjammers. People began to ask about a new German mercantile marine. Where would the future captains and officers come from if there were no more sailing ships in which they could learn the ropes and get their training?

Shipping regulations in Germany still required that a candidate for a helmsman's papers and even a master's certificate must have done a certain amount of training in sailing ships whose total area of canvas was at least twice the ship's length multiplied by the beam. The *Pamir* and the *Passat,* each with a minimum area of canvas of about 2,800 square meters, possessed these requirements, and there were no other qualified craft anywhere in Germany.

Finally, a Hamburg shipowner named Schlieven bought both craft and, after having them modernized, engaged them as cargo sailing ships to train the future officers of the merchant navy. Thus the *Pamir* and *Passat* were brought back to Germany, refitted, and equipped with all the latest devices.

Carrying a 900-h.p. Krupp-Diesel engine as auxiliary, the *Pamir* sailed under the German flag again after thirty-eight years. On January 10, 1952, she left Hamburg on her first voyage, bound for Rio de Janeiro.

Almost before she was out to sea she met trouble at the eastern entrance to the English Channel when, during a storm, the screw of her auxiliary engine fell off and she lost an anchor. The storm developed rapidly, turning into a gale which gave the forty-nine cadets aboard a real taste of danger. They watched as two British ships came to the aid of the *Pamir*. She put over her remaining anchor, the flukes caught, and the immediate danger had passed. Better weather soon followed, but the incident brought back to the older officers an earlier disaster which ended in death at sea for many German sailing cadets when the Hapag training ship *Admiral Karpfanger,* a 2,853-ton four-masted steel bark of Hamburg, sailed from Port Germein, South Australia, for Falmouth, England, on February 8, 1938, and vanished at sea. Forty German sailing cadets were aboard, and there was great grief when it was realized that the boys would never return.

Aboard the *Pamir* on her trip to South America there were no further incidents of danger, and after thirty-four days at sea, she sailed into Rio. Necessary repairs had been made out on the ocean. As she came up the bay the German training ship with her Cadets received a great welcome.

Unfortunately, on October 30, 1952, when the *Pamir* reached Rotterdam at the end of her second South American voyage, she was impounded by a Dutch ship's chandler. Schlieven was in financial trouble. Not only had he sunk all his capital into the purchase and refitting of the two sailing ships, but he had also amassed a considerable number of other debts, and his vessels were not earning the amount of money he had expected. Finally a bank foreclosed, and for two years the *Pamir* and *Passat* remained at their moorings.

A *Pamir* and *Passat* fund was opened in 1955 to get the two craft sailing the high seas again, and sufficient money was raised to buy them. Both were put into service again in 1956 as training ships. On June 1, 1957, the *Pamir* sailed from Hamburg on her sixteenth round trip to the Argentine. At this time she was one of the most stable sailing ships which have ever put to sea, with six watertight compartments, new steel masts, and sixteen-millimeter iron plates.

Captain Hermann Eggers, who had already made seven trips in the *Pamir*, had planned to command the voyage, but a sudden family crisis made him decide to go on leave. In his place sailed Captain Johannes Diebitsch, a mariner of extensive knowledge and experience. When the *Pamir* started back to Europe from Buenos Aires the ship was supposedly in perfect shape and there was no apparent cause for anxiety.

On September 20 Captain Diebitsch received a warning of a hurricane which the United States weather bureau had christened Carrie. It is believed that he then attempted to sail around the storm. Contrary to all expectations, however, Carrie did not veer to port as a normal hurricane would do. Instead, the mighty gale headed for the central Atlantic and caught the *Pamir*, battering the tall-masted ship, which was under full press of sail and on a northerly course homeward at the time. She was unable to ride out the blow and sank to the bottom of the sea.

What will always be an unsolved mystery is how Captain Diebitsch and Chief Mate Rolf Dieter Köhler planned to meet the situation when they realized hurricane Carrie was going to catch them. We shall never know, as neither of them survived and the log books went to the bottom with the *Pamir*.

On board the sailing craft was Captain Fred Schmidt, a writer of sea stories. For years he had taught in the navigation school at Lübeck. Schmidt signed on for this particular voyage to take pictures for an illustrated work he was writing on life in ocean-going sailing ships.

His last letter, written an hour before leaving Buenos Aires, is full of enthusiasm for the vessel and her crew. He was already looking forward to publishing the photographs and articles at the end of the voyage. The hurricane caught the *Pamir* that Sunday evening and destroyed all Schmidt's plans for the future. The fate of many of the other individuals aboard the *Pamir* will never be known because those who survived only saw events in their own particular area of action.

On Sunday, the twenty-first of September, 1957, at 1500 hours Greenwich time, the *Pamir* sent out an SOS that she was in a heavy gale. Her position was given as 35° 57' N., 40° 20' W. She stated that she had a 45 degree list, was in danger of sinking, and all her sails were lost. The British coast radio station at Portishead rebroadcast the message at once so that all available craft could reach the scene.

Ships within a near radius hurried to the spot after receiving the SOS. The closest of all was the American freighter *President Taylor*. Her radio operator announced to the world that she was making full speed for the *Pamir* and hoped to arrive at 2300 hours that night.

The Canadian destroyer *Crusader* then radioed that she would arrive on the scene within twelve hours. The *Manchester Trader,* a British steamer, picked up an SOS, and immediately relayed it to all other stations. Shortly after this the *Trader* received a broken message which stated in part that the *Pamir* had her ". . . foremast smashed by the heavy sea."

Nothing further from the *Pamir*'s radio was ever heard. Other craft announced their plans and positions. The British tanker *San Silvester* signaled that the *President Taylor* was due at the scene at 2300 hours, and the *Penn Trader* expected to arrive at the same time. The Norwegian motor tanker *Jaguar* was 160 miles NNW, making eight knots. The German motor ship *Nordsee* was making ten knots, and the British motor ship *Hauraki* was proceeding at fifteen knots. The *Tacoma Star* and the Dutch ocean-going tug, *Swarte Zee* also started for the sinking *Pamir*.

It had been eight o'clock that Sunday evening when the *Pamir*'s captain received the final warning that a hurricane could be expected within two hours.

A survivor explained:

We were given orders to secure all rigging. All hands were sent aloft, but before we could start taking in sail the hurricane overwhelmed us.

Captain Diebitsch's order to trim sails came too late. A mighty squall tore the foresails away, and the mast snapped. From that moment disaster followed disaster. Things went so quickly that no one could say exactly what happened. The power of the storm forced the ship over on her side. We took on a 30° list, which increased to 35°, and finally to 40°, the limit of the instrument's recording device. Of course, by this time the decks and holds were awash. The order, "All hands on deck," was given. We all put on our lifesaving jackets; the ship heeled over more and more, shivering beneath the weight of mountainous seas. No longer could we get a foothold on the almost vertical deck, and it was impossible to lower a lifeboat with this heavy list. We held on fast to the rail on the starboard side for the port side was already underwater.

When our ship suddenly capsized we plunged down into

the water, one after the other. Many of the boys must have been drowned at this moment. Those with any strength left attempted to swim away, but the suction of the ship drew us after her. Our only thought was to get away from her.

Now it was every man for himself. Small groups reached pieces of wreckage, to which they clung. There were fifteen men in my group. At last we sighted an empty boat drifting ahead of us. It took me an hour to swim to it, and only nine others reached it. We clung fast to the boat while the heavy seas broke over us. After long weary efforts, we managed to climb into the lifeboat, which was full of water, kept floating by its ballast tanks.

Meanwhile, shortly after eleven that evening the *President Taylor* and the *Penn Trader* arrived at the position the *Pamir* had given. They did not know if it was correct. In the dark, stormy night it was in any case extremely difficult for the two cargo boats to find the damaged vessel. They cruised about the area looking for the ship or her shipwrecked crew.

The *Tacoma Star,* a Blue Star Liner, now arrived in the area. A few minutes before midnight, lights were sighted in the distance by the *Penn Trader,* but nothing was found. Soon after this lights appeared at another location, but disappeared again. The report of flashing lights sighted traveled around the world over the air, arousing new hopes. Since the *Pamir*'s radio had become silent, it was feared she had gone down with all hands. Shortly before dawn the Canadian destroyer *Crusader* arrived to help in the search. The hours went by, but the searchlights from four ships found nothing.

The world hoped that the *Pamir* might have been driven before the storm with her radio out of action. A broken foremast, which the *Pamir* had announced, was no reason to fear the worst, but the *Pamir* had reported a 45-degree list, and this was the real cause for alarm.

When daylight came that Sunday the air sea rescue squadron station on the Azores and the coast guard cutter *Astacan* began a search of the sea west and northwest of the Azores, but bad weather and poor visibility forced the abandonment of it before anything was sighted. Apparently the *Pamir* had disappeared with all hands, and not the slightest trace remained to tell of her fate.

At noon the British coast guard station at Portishead in Somerset, England, relayed a message from the tanker *San Silvester* that she had sighted an empty lifeboat and taken it aboard. Badly damaged, it bore the name Lübeck, the *Pamir*'s home port. The rudder of the lifeboat was still lashed inside, and it was apparent that it had been washed overboard. Two more lifeboats were sighted that afternoon, but the stormy Sunday came to an end without a single member of the crew having been found.

Then, late at night, the American freighter *Saxon* sighted a lifeboat. As they drew closer, they counted five sailors still aboard, the remaining members of the ten who had clambered into the craft some hours earlier. The boat was full of water, as it could not be bailed out because of the stormy weather. Details of the rescue of these five lucky survivors went all over the world, and it was now certain from what the cadets told their rescuers that the *Pamir* had foundered in hurricane Carrie.

The survivors told those aboard the freighter that only a small number, had ever been able to take to the boats. There had only been two lifeboats available, because of the terrible angle of list on the *Pamir*. They explained how their five companions had washed overboard one by one, unable to retain their hold. The survivors estimated that there had been twenty-five men in the second lifeboat. As her lights had been sighted briefly just before the five men had been rescued, they guessed that the second boat could not be far away.

Strangely enough, twenty-four hours went by without a single report from the other craft. Meanwhile, it was erroneously announced to the world by a careless radio operator that forty survivors had been rescued.

The ships kept up their hunt for the remaining sailors and cadets. Finally, the United States Coast Guard cutter *Absecon* sighted the missing lifeboat. Sadly enough, only one man was in her, and he was quickly rescued.

The sole survivor told a dramatic story of how the others had been panicked into swimming to a waiting vessel whose men did not see the lifeboat. The ship seemed just a short distance away, but when they leaped into the water and started to swim, she steamed off, slowly at first. With all twenty-four men in the sea swimming desperately, the vessel gathered speed and disappeared into the gathering darkness. The sailors and cadets drowned one by one as the remaining occupant of the lifeboat watched helplessly.

He proved to be the last survivor to be saved. Eighty-one men and boys lost their lives. Nothing else is known concerning the *Pamir* and her unhappy fate out on the Atlantic Ocean.

CHAPTER 22

The *Revonoc*

On Wednesday, January 1, 1958, the forty-four-foot yawl
Revonoc II * left the port of Key West in Florida with five
people aboard bound for Miami. They were millionaire
yachtsman Harvey Conover, who was then sixty-five years of
age; his wife Dorothy, sixty; their son Lawrence, twenty-seven;
and a passenger, William Fluegelman of Scarsdale, N.Y., a
textile executive. Mrs. Fluegelman at the last minute decided
not to go as she was susceptible to seasickness. The yawl proceeded out to sea, and Captain Conover exchanged the usual
signals and greetings with other craft as they passed.

The very next morning a gigantic weather disturbance hit
the area. The *Revonoc*, a long distance from her Miami destination, was probably in the middle of this rapidly forming
hurricane, and she was never heard from again.

Every person aboard the yawl was an expert sailor. Con-

---

* *Revonoc* stands for Conover spelled backwards. Extremely well built, the
wooden-hulled *Revonoc* had only the finest materials in her construction. She
had outside lead ballast, a bronze centerboard, and two aluminum masts.

over himself had won the Miami to Nassau race on no less than three occasions and was considered by many to be the outstanding yachtsman of his generation.

Not only were the members of the *Revonoc*'s crew superb sailors, but the yawl herself represented the very last word in construction. Designed six months before by Sparkman and Stevens, the *Revonoc* was rightly called Conover's dream ship. Costing $85,000, she was built not only for comfort but for safety. In fact the designers were of the opinion that the *Revonoc* was the safest craft afloat. Robert Sparkman, even after he learned that the *Revonoc* was missing, stated confidently that she should come through the storm without foundering. As the days went by and the yawl was unreported, Harvey Conover's friends still clung to the thought that he was too good a sailor with too good a boat to worry about.

A careful study of that Thursday's storm reveals that it began to rain heavily in Miami about ten o'clock that morning, and two hours later the wind was in the north gusting at thirty knots. The *Revonoc* had then been sailing more than a full day but could not possibly reach Miami against the wind. Unfortunately, weather reports on the storm had not been given out in advance, and were released only after the wind velocity had become dangerous. Thus, it was not until almost three o'clock on Thursday afternoon, when the terrific rain battered its way into Miami, that boatmen in general realized a storm of dangerous proportions was about to hit the area. At three o'clock the weather bureau advisory stated:

"Hoist gale warnings, 3 P.M. Thursday, Palm Beach southward to Dry Tortugas."

In this way the people of Florida learned that what proved

to be the worst storm in the winter history of Miami was on the way, but the warning was too late to help Harvey Conover and his unlucky crew. That night great mile-a-minute winds battered the Miami shore, and for several hours the full hurricane lashed the coast at seventy-miles an hour, ripping apart awnings and blowing out windows. Debris from the ocean washed high on Miami's shores, and every section of the city suffered substantial damage. Gigantic waves swept through the Gulf Stream, and the storm (which was later labeled a fluke) blew so hard that boatmen were in trouble before they realized it. The almost universal complaint was that sufficient warning had not been given.

Richard Bertram,* a close associate of Conover's, now became worried when his friend was not heard from, and on Saturday called the Miami coast guard. His call started one of the greatest air and sea searches Florida ever experienced. The coast guard reported the next day that the *Revonoc* must have been caught in the storm, since a check of all the ports had failed to discover her and the search planes also reported in the negative.

On January 6 the twelve-foot sailing dinghy *Revonoc Junior* was found on the beach near Jupiter Inlet Light† about eighty-two miles north of Miami. It was reported that the skiff probably had been pulled from its mountings by a wave which had swept right over the yawl.

On that same January 6 a craft was seen stranded at an island beach, Gun Cay, about sixty miles east of Miami, and hopes were strong that she was the missing *Revonoc*. A rescue

* Others associated with the strenuous efforts to find the missing yacht included Henry duPont and Rod Stephens.

† Jupiter Light is at the mouth of the Loxahatchee River. Built in 1860, it was rebuilt to a height of 146 feet in 1930, and now has a radio beacon.

group which went ashore found, however, that she was not Harvey Conover's yacht. She was identified by the coast guard as the *Hootmon,* a forty-foot yawl that ran aground during a storm the previous Thursday. She had been chartered by a party of eight from the Coral Reef Yacht Club, who were taken off the island by a civilian craft.

Three planes continued a search of the area from Delray Beach to Fort Pierce and eastward past the Bahamas. The section between the west shore of Andros Island in the Bahamas and the lower Florida east coast was also carefully covered with no results. In all, twenty-seven planes searched for the missing yawl, and 100,000 square miles of ocean was subjected to the sea hunt.

Mr. Conover was president of the Conover-Nast Publications, Inc., of New York, which published *Aviation Age* and other technical magazines. He had been a World War I pilot in the air corps.

In spite of the hurricane Richard Bertram still thought that the *Revonoc* had survived the gale. A shrimp boat had been towed into Miami after staying afloat during the worst of the gale, even though she had lost engine power. Her captain told the coast guard that he had seen no other boats of any type, but for some reason he later changed his story and claimed that he had seen a white boat capsized with several people clinging to it.

The coast guard and the Cuban navy united in the search, continuing a constant patrol until January 13. Then came a report from the captain of a sixty-five foot cruiser sailing from Key West to Miami, who stated that he had run aground near East Washerwoman Light off Marathon, Florida, where the chart indicated he was in deep water. Glancing to the stern he found that he had hit an underwater obstruction, a craft which had gone down as the result of what appeared to be an explosion. His cruiser finally slid over the object in the rising tide but sustained damage. He succeeded in starting one engine, however, and was able to reach Miami.

It was believed that Conover's yacht might have been the obstruction, but a dragging operation begun in the area failed utterly to prove what it was.

As the years have gone by, nothing in addition to the craft's dinghy has ever been found, and the loss of the *Revonoc* remains one of the unsolved mysteries of the sea.

~~~~~~~~~~

~~~~~~~~~~

~~~~~~~~~~

CHAPTER 23

Island of Lost Ships

Blinding raindrops pelted and splattered against our cockpit windshield, slithered in neat little rows along its surface, and flipped off into space. Through the steel-gray atmosphere of the storm we could see 700 feet below us the breaking crests of gigantic waves. The mighty Atlantic was putting on a spectacular show. With any sort of luck an airplane can fly through or around a rain-laden gale without mishap. But our task was far more difficult.

We wanted to find Sable Island, a narrow stretch of sand bar 150 miles off the coast of Nova Scotia known as the graveyard of the North Atlantic. Unless we bored through the fog, mist, and rain almost directly above the island we might miss it entirely.

We were getting more discouraged by the minute. Ray Hylan, pilot of our two-engined Grumman Widgeon amphibian, photographer Jerry Fund, and I had left the Marshfield, Massachusetts, airport the day before full of hope and confidence. We had been promised good weather, but now we were being buffeted by a substantial storm. Try as we would, we could not catch even a glimpse of our destination. We were just floundering around far out to sea. I told Ray about my first visit with Major Paul Dudley to Sable Island a few years before, but it did not seem to cheer him up.*

With ice threatening and conditions getting worse momentarily, we decided time and again to give up the search and return to the mainland. But the gale was apparently testing us. As soon as we turned shoreward, the rain would moderate; when we turned seaward again, the storm resumed its full fury.

Sable Island has been a mariner's graveyard ever since man first sailed the ocean lanes. It is estimated that no fewer than 10,000 lives and 506 craft of all kinds have been lost on its terrifying reefs, bars, beaches, and sand spits. The island lies one-quarter of the way between New York and Cape Finisterre, Spain. Mariners say that its sands are like a chameleon, quickly taking on the varying colors of the surrounding ocean. A ship may come to grief on this camouflaged sand spit before the captain realizes that he is in trouble.

It is hard to comprehend the awesome isolation of this thin strand of sand. On its shores pirates, beachcombers, murderers, and convicts have taken their stand against the elements. Even today it remains as a menacing sentinel of sand—at once a threat to and a guardian of ships and planes. Owned by Canada, Sable Island now has two lighthouses, a lifesaving station, a radio station, a radiosonde station, and a weather station. Officers manning these outposts take their families to the island, but no one else is allowed to live there. We

* See my *Mysteries and Adventures along the Atlantic Coast*, pp. 37–38.

wanted to find out what life was like on this ominous, forlorn wasteland.

Flying in that tempest of the sky far above the ocean, our danger was not in being caught in Sable's sands, but in missing them altogether. Just as we were about to abandon our efforts, however, there was a sudden unaccountable lull in the gale. A partial clearing developed, and soon we flew entirely out of the storm under an overcast of 1,500 feet.

Almost at once we could see a ridge of breaking, crested waves, shattering as they struck barely submerged sand bars. More important, off to the left were sand dunes and beaches. Finally we saw the reassuring buildings and red-and-white lighthouse of Sable Island itself.

Flying at 500 feet over the eastern end of the island, we looked down for a moment on the wreck of the ill-fated *Gale,* a New England trawler lost in 1945, and then headed west. As we flew over the southern beach, the roar of our engines scattered several hundred seals and sent them scrambling into the water. A minute later we passed directly over a herd of wild horses. Then we flew almost at masthead level above the wreck of the Greek freighter *Alpheus,* lost in 1941, and the two masts and submerged hull of the *Manhasset,* a more recent victim of Sable Island's sands.

We buzzed Wallace Lake, a salt pond seven miles long near the western end of the island. Then, banking sharply at a point just over the wreck of a Liberator bomber, we flew in cater-cornered from the southwest to make a perfect landing on the lake.

As we taxied toward the eastern end of the lake, two wagons came forward to meet us—one a buckboard affair and the other a long flat platform cart on which rode a dory. Pushing our wheels down, we hit the sand flats in knee-deep water and, with a thundering roar, brought the plane high and dry on the shore less than fifty feet from the startled islanders. They all rushed toward us, and we spilled out of the plane to acknowledge their geetings.*

The first to shake hands was Superintendent Clifford Russell Faulkner. Closely following were Ralph Newell, officer in charge of the radiosonde division, and the island's foreman, Willard Langille. Others crowding about the plane included all the rest of the twenty men on the island except those on duty, as well as all three women residents—Mrs. Katy Tzagarakis, housekeeper for the superintendent; Mrs. Eileen Maxner, wife of Radio Officer Stuart Maxner; and Mrs. Muriel Newell, wife of the radiosonde officer. The island's three children, Stephen Maxner, five, Carolyn Maxner, three, and two-year-old Deryl Newell, were also there to greet us.

All who could jammed aboard the two wagons for the trip to one of the island's three settlements. There are no roads on Sable Island, merely paths through the sand dunes just wide enough for the teams of partly tamed wild horses. It was up hill and down dale for more than two miles to the radiosonde station.

After freshening up at the Newell home, we were taken on an inspection tour of the station. There balloons are sent aloft bearing instruments which automatically send back reports on pressure, humidity, and temperature.

We called next at the superintendent's home, where Mrs. Tzagarakis, the housekeeper, had prepared a meal for us. Over coffee, she told us of her life on Sable Island.

---

* Thus I became the only person from the United States ever to have flown to Sable Island twice.

"I like it here," she said. "First of all it's very healthy, and then everyone is so nice to me. The Department of Education sends out films every so often, and we all have nice get-togethers on Sunday nights. In the summer we can swim, and there's always plenty of horseback riding. As you can easily guess, hiking is popular as well."

Leaving the house, we climbed back aboard the buckboard to ride to the western end of the island, where the sandy hills are slowly washing away. Eleven buildings are still standing there, among them the former residence of the superintendent, but all have been abandoned.

Charts dating back to 1766 show Sable is traveling eastward at the average rate of one eighth of a mile a year, having moved 22½ miles farther out to sea from Halifax in 197 years.

People who attempt to visit Sable Island by sea must plan for the possibility that they may be away from home for months. During the last century customs officer James Miller obtained fourteen days' leave to inspect goods salvaged on the island. In attempting to land, three of his party were drowned, leaving only one other man with Miller on the schooner. Then the wind drove the vessel hundreds of miles to the south. Eventually, running before the wind, the schooner reached Antigua in the Leeward Islands. Returning to Nova Scotia by packet four months after he had left on fourteen days' leave, Miller discovered that he had been given up as lost at sea.

Even today the great breakers all around the harborless island make it dangerous to go ashore from the sea. The present supply craft occasionally has been forced to wait off the island for as long as seventeen days, unable to land her goods because of high seas. A return from this outpost of the Atlantic also is perilous. On October 18, 1870, the island supply craft *Ocean Traveller* left for the mainland with Sable Island families on leave and was never heard from again.

On rare occasions men on the island have starved to death. One year there was no boat from August 6 until a few days before Christmas, and the suffering was intense. Even as late as 1926 residents were down to a limited supply of bread, crackers, and molasses. Perhaps the grimmest Sable Island starvation story of all came to light eighty years ago, when rusty guns, bayonets, broken glass, fragments of pottery, and a tattered British ensign were found. They apparently were relics of a sixteenth-century shipwreck before the island was populated. Several coins of the Elizabethan age were uncovered, together with fragments of animal and human bones. Evidently cannibalism broke out before the last survivor died.

Sometimes shipwrecked crews, instead of showing gratitude for being rescued, have mutinied. In the mid-nineteenth century the captain of a wrecked ship raised his gun to shoot Superintendent McKenna but was quickly disarmed by other government men. On another occasion sixteen shipwrecked men attacked the islanders, but in a terrible fist fight they were subdued by government officers.

Winds and sand obliterate everything on Sable Island in time. A full-rigged American clipper ship is encased in one gigantic ninety-foot sand dune; the wind built up the dune until even the rigging and the main truck were covered. In spite of shelter fences and other obstructions, the sand sweeps in over buildings, wrecks, graveyards, and everything else man-made. Recent shipwrecks vanish into the sand overnight, while others buried for hundreds of years are suddenly swept clean of their century-old covering.

Only eight craft out of the more than 500 lost around the island have ever been freed from Sable's sands. The most unusual case was that of the ship *Myrtle*. Wrecked and abandoned on January 11, 1840, she freed herself in another storm two months later and drifted across to Fayal in the Azores, arriving the following July. The vessel was repaired and put back in service.

Frank Tanner, cook for the island workers, has a wealth of information about the Sable Island wrecks. "I've been out here several times," he told me. "In 1941, I was lighthouse keeper for the East Light, and I was there when a Hudson bomber with five American fliers hit the radio tower that June." Lost in a bad gale, the pilot and four other airmen were killed instantly. The crash, which came at a time when Lockheed Hudsons were being ferried to Europe, was probably caused by the pilot riding the Sable Island radio beam too long. The men are buried in nameless graves at the island cemetery.

"I'll also never forget the wreck of the *Independence Hall*," Tanner went on. "She was a big ship from Philadelphia, and nine men perished. She hit in early afternoon and two hours later had broken apart. Only three bodies ever came ashore, and I picked them up eighteen miles from where the wreck took place.

"It's always interesting to hike along the beach, for you never know what you'll find. Sometimes the only way we know a ship has gone down is when we find an oar or a life preserver. At one time the station was crowded with such souvenirs.

"Dying men have been sighted drifting in open boats by Sable Island. I wasn't here then, but I hear tell that once three Frenchmen came ashore in a dory. Lost while fishing, they'd gone eleven days without food or water. Their tongues stuck out of their mouths and were black, but they recovered.

"Then there was Fred Wilson, from the American schooner *Commonwealth*, at sea for six days alone in a small dory. Making Sable Island in a northwest gale, he was unable to land, and the surfboat was sent out. He was just like the Frenchmen, with his blackened tongue hanging from his mouth, but he also lived.

"One man landed from a wreck no one ever saw, got as far as the Old Sailors' Home, opened his mouth to speak, and dropped dead. The man and the wreck were never identified."

Many of the men working on Sable have found unusual and valuable articles on the beach. A resident of the bunkhouse, where sixteen men live, has a collection of walrus tusks, quarter boards from ships, life preservers, and coins.

"There must be two million dollars in buried and sunken treasure around here," Tanner told me. Every ship or craft of any sort always carried its strongbox, and some of the vessels were well-heeled for trading purposes. All that money is aboard wrecks around the island and it's waiting for lucky finders."

Among the lucky finders, I was told, was one P. S. Dodd. The exact amount of his discovery, made in 1884, was not known, but it was sufficient—even after he gave the Canadian government half—for him to return to the mainland and start a real estate business in Halifax. Another islander, whose name no one could recall, once found a bundle of 200 five-pound Bank of England notes worth about $5,000. He also retired from the service and went to the mainland with his wealth.

When we returned to the radiosonde station, I visited another of the three women on the island. Mrs. Muriel Newell told me she had come to Sable on August 17, 1953, and her first glimpse of her future home was at 6:00 A.M. from a porthole of the supply ship *Cornwallis*. Because the water is shallow all round the island, a supply surfboat took her and her eleven-months-old son Deryl the remaining mile ashore through the breakers. She was reunited with her husband at the water's edge.

"After the supply ship had departed, I started my duties as cook for my husband and the three other young men who make up the personnel of the radiosonde station," she said. "This keeps me rather busy, but we do have a sort of holiday when the supply boats arrive, about four times a year. At other times we women on the island manage to arrange our work so that we can walk on the beach, where once I shot a seal. We also get together for an afternoon of horseback riding and other recreation whenever we can.

"All of our personal shopping has to be done by mail approximately three months in advance. As there are no doctors or nurses here, we also have to act as our own medical advisers in case of accidents."

Sable's third woman resident, Mrs. Eileen Maxner, told me that her two children miss the company of other playmates. "Television helps them realize they will enjoy other children when they return to the mainland," she said. "They talk quite frequently to their friends and relatives via short-wave radio.

"The food situation has improved quite a bit since my last trip out here seven years ago. Frozen meats were unheard of here at that time. Now we have meat all the year round, which adds to our menu variety."

Fishing is frowned upon because of the treacherous surf which breaks on the three great barrier reefs surrounding the island. But if there is a shipwreck, the lifesaving crew quickly launches a surfboat and rows out through the breakers.

There have been many thrilling rescues at Sable Island. When we visited the old lifesaving station barn, we were deeply impressed by the many shipwreck mementos housed there. Nailed in every conceivable spot—on the wall, on the giant wooden girders, and on the smaller timbers as well—were countless quarter boards and side boards from ill-fated vessels.

Sable Island could almost be known as the headquarters for unsolved mysteries of the sea. Of course, because of the 506 ships wrecked there it is known as "the graveyard of the Atlantic," but in actuality there are many other locations which could also bear the same title. Nevertheless, that grim, ghost-haunted fragment of sand, strewn with more wrecks than any other twenty miles of the earth's surface, lies so flat on the sea that on an overcast day it is hardly distinguishable from the surrounding ocean. It is a deadly ambush for ships, for all around it is a tangle of inner, middle, and outer shoals ever feeding on wrecks.

The Far North dispatches its icy current to meet and deflect the Gulf Stream, creating scores of confusing flows and eddies. It is almost certain death if the crew of a vessel, at the height of a great storm, sees the breakers of Sable Island rising at them like watery ghosts in their dance of death, to the accompaniment of the whistling of the wind.

I recall the bell of one of the wrecked ships which was used to call the men, women, and children to worship under the leadership of the superintendent of the island. He conducted the services, using a capstan for a lectern.

A church service at Sable Island is never to be forgotten by the visitor. The background noise of the rote of the sea, the childlike cries of the sea gulls, and the shrill whistle of the wind make a deep impression on the minds of the visitors.

This so-called graveyard of the Atlantic belongs to Nova Scotia, and lies 150 miles from Halifax and 85 miles east of Cape Canso. It is a treeless, shrubless waste, seamed by wind and wave and ever changing. A cone-shaped hill near the east end, once a mere undulation of sand, is now over a hundred feet high, and is still growing. Other hillocks are gradually being moved away by storms. The sand dunes are liable to be undermined and swept out of existence so swiftly that they are carefully watched from the various stations on the island, there being no certainty how far an inroad of the sea will extend after each successful attack.

I told the Sable Islanders of Gustav Kobbé, whom I have mentioned in several of my other books. Kobbé visited Sable Island shortly before 1900, and wrote of his experiences later in *Ainslee's Magazine*.

Even the coarse grass of the island grows in a different manner from that of the mainland. It does not bear seed, but shoots up from roots which run along under the sand. During the winter the sand is blown over the grass, and buries it sometimes three or four feet deep. But the hardy blades grow up the next season, as if the island sands had protected them from the cold of the winter in order to make them all the stronger.

The shores of this long, narrow island are formed by two parallel bow-shaped ridges of sand, enclosing a low valley, eight miles of which is occupied by a shallow salt-water lake. The first authentic information concerning this lake shows that it had an opening to the sea on its north side, and that it was considerably longer than it now is. The opening was closed by a heavy storm, which filled it up with sand. Then another storm more violent than its predecessor broke two openings through the beach, one of which was large enough for the passage of small vessels, for which the lake afforded a good harbor. But it seems as if, after all, the island had only been laying a trap for the unwary. For in 1836, just after two vessels had entered the lake, a severe storm closed the inlets and imprisoned the vessels. In 1881, a gale opened a narrow gulch at the east end, and the lake then shrank to its present dimensions. In heavy storms the sea now rushed over the sand-bar which forms the south side of the lake. In one such storm the *Mereta* was carried over two bars and over the beach into the lake. The salvage of this vessel was a remarkably skillful piece of work.

A government station has been on Sable Island since 1802. The main station is three miles from the West End Light, and near it is a lookout tower. The number of people at Sable Island is often swelled by the crews and passengers of wrecked vessels who are obliged to remain until the semiannual visit of the supply steamer. The only good landing place is on the north side, and even there a landing can be effected only under favorable conditions, as the goverment steamer cannot come closer in than a mile. Once eight days were spent trying to send a boat ashore.

Near the main station is a house where wrecked seamen are cared for. A lifesaving station with a lifeboat and a rocket apparatus stand nearby. On this part of the island live the superintendent and six or eight men. Three other stations are located about four miles apart. Most of the wrecks occur at the east end, where two lifeboats are maintained, one on the north, the other on the south side. In addition to the stations which have lifeboats and crews, there are several houses of refuge, stocked with provisions and fuel for castaways who may be unable to make their way to the stations.

The history of Sable Island opens with a tragedy. This sand bar, with all its attendant horrors of desolation, figures early in Colonial history, for Sable Island was the site of the first settlement of what is now British North America. In 1534 Jacques Cartier discovered Acadia, and brought such glowing accounts of it back to France, that the king decided to establish a colony there. He appointed Roberval as lieutenant general of Canada, but the expedition proved a failure.

Sir Humphrey Gilbert's attempt to establish a colony in Newfoundland also failed. One of his vessels, *The Admiral,* was lost on Sable Island, and he, with another of the remaining two ships, went down during a storm on the Grand Banks. The account of the loss of *The Admiral* which has come down to us speaks of the "flats and dangers" in which the vessels found themselves enmeshed on their approach to Sable Island. The doomed ship continued sounding trumpets and guns. Then "Strange voices from the deep scared the helmsman from his post on board the frigate." The other two vessels beat over the northwest bar, and the record of their soundings given in the narrative reads the same as if the disaster had occurred but yesterday. One hundred men were lost with *The Admiral,* this disaster forming a ghastly beginning to the many stories of shipwrecks which have occurred on Sable Island.

In 1598 the Marquis de la Roche, who had been appointed lieutenant general and viceroy of Canada, set sail with forty-eight convicts. His first landfall was Sable Island. Instead of sailing on toward the mainland, he anchored off the island and set the convicts ashore for safekeeping, he himself intending meanwhile to select a place of settlement on the mainland. But stress of weather caused his plan to miscarry. He was compelled to weigh anchor and sail back to France. There he was seized and imprisoned by creditors, and it was not until five years later that an expedition was fitted out to visit the island and ascertain what had become of the convicts.

Of the forty-eight who had been set ashore, only eleven remained. At first they had fought with one another, and several were killed. At last, finding that by concerted action they could make better provision for survival, they made peace with one another. From a Spanish galleon wreck—for even in those days there were wrecks on Sable Island—they obtained timber for a rough shelter and a few sheep. There was plenty of driftwood for fuel along the shores of the island. De la Roche had left some agricultural implements, and with these they tilled a small, sheltered valley called to this day the "French Gardens." When they had been carried back to France and were brought before the king, clad in rough sealskins and presenting a pitiable sight, the king relented toward them, pardoned them, and settled a sum of money on each. Strange to say, these men elected to return to the island, where for many years they did a thriving trade in the skins and ivory of walruses, which in those days came to the island in large numbers.

The loss of Sir Humphrey Gilbert's *Admiral* at Sable Island was but the beginning of many such horrors. As shipping increased, Sable Island became the scene of countless acts of villainy. In summer, bands of wreckers from the mainland settled there, lured ships ashore, and not only despoiled the dead, but killed and robbed those who survived the perils of shipwreck.

If the gruesome records of Sable Island were all known it would be found that it has been the scene of numberless crimes. Those very dangers of the sea which brought victims to the moon-cussers and pirates who infested the island protected them against interference while they carried out their horrible murders. Soon sea captains began to ask themselves whether it was worse at Sable Island to die in the great surf or to be killed later by the cutthroats. Think of the poor castaway staggering from the watery grave which had almost claimed him, only to be struck down by the knife or bludgeon of the murderers of Sable Island.

For many years the island with its natural horrors—the fogs, storms, currents, and shoals—reached out like the tentacles of a devilfish, to pile up on these sandy shores the bloody work of pirates and wreckers. Worse than anything else was the fact that piracy continued unavenged. In the spring men who were worse than pirates would set sail from villages in New England and Canada, to return in the fall with rich cargoes of silk, jewelry, and even gold. Where their treasures had been obtained no one knew, but of one thing all were sure. It was ill-gotten gain; and when neighbors shook their head and whispered low, as one of these returned voyagers passed by, mention of Sable Island was never omitted.

Shortly after the turn of the nineteenth century there occurred on the island a double catastrophe so great that people on the mainland no longer dared content themselves with merely looking on and doing nothing. In 1801 the British transport *Amelia*, officers, recruits, and crew numbering 200, was wrecked on Sable Island. Every soul but one was lost, and the single survivor was put to death by the wreckers on the island. Sent out to search for possible survivors, a schooner was also lost on the island. The single survivor of this second disaster brought back with him a story which established as facts the horrors that had only been surmised. The government now took over Sable Island. As a result, the nucleus of the present stations was established, and since then no one has been permitted to live on the island without a government license.

But while this precaution put a stop to crimes of man against man, the story of shipwreck has kept apace with the ever-recurring fogs and storms. A carefully maintained record shows that since the establishment of the government station more than 200 vessels and 4,700 lives have been lost on Sable Island. Add to these the disasters which occurred before the station was established, and those which have happened since but have remained unknown, and the record is simply appalling. The island is literally framed with the ribs of lost ships.

"Strange voices from the deep" frightened the helmsman on one of the ships of Sir Humphrey Gilbert's squadron. Strange voices from the deep still add to the accumulation of horrors of a storm on Sable Island. The long slender bar of sand vibrates from end to end to the thunder of the surf. Even old residents in great storms often find it impossible to sleep. The wind strips the ghastly remnants of wrecks of their sandy covering. Seizing the bleached skeletons of castaways, it lifts them to their bony feet to confront with grinning skulls and clattering arms the patrol who is toiling through the gale. The record of disaster is everywhere, and it can be said that every foot of the island is haunted.

One of the strangest legends dates from the wreck of the *Amelia*. There is just enough evidence of truth connected with it to show what bloody deeds were added on that occasion to the terrors of shipwreck. Captain Torrens, who commanded the schooner which was dispatched to Sable Island after the wreck of the *Amelia*, was one of the survivors of the second disaster. A passenger on the lost transport was Mrs. Copeland, on her way to join her husband. The captain had been told that Mrs. Copeland wore on her forefinger a ring of peculiar nature.

The story has it that Captain Torrens, wandering over the island one night in search of possible survivors, was attracted by the piteous whining of his dog in front of a small, open shelter, known to have existed at that time but long since toppled to pieces. Approaching the shelter, he was startled to see the figure of a woman holding toward him the bleeding stump of a forefinger. While he was gazing at the apparition, it rose, silently glided past him and went into the sea. But time and again thereafter the woman with the missing finger has been seen wandering over the sand hills.*

It is probably only part of the weird legend that Captain

* I tell the story in detail in *Mysteries and Adventures along the Atlantic Coast*, pp. 33–37.

Torrens, feeling sure that a shocking crime had been committed, tracked the guilty pirate until he discovered his family on the coast of Labrador and learned that the ring had been sold in Halifax. It is a fact, however, that many years after the disaster, Mrs. Copeland's ring was discovered in a jewelry store in Halifax and was returned to her family.

One of the apparitions which is said to walk the night is the ghost of a French nobleman. The king fell in love with the nobleman's wife and took the surest means of getting rid of the husband forever by banishing him to Sable Island. This unusual ghost shows himself only to French castaways, to whom it is said he always complains bitterly of the king.

The ghost of the drowned lifesaver, appearing during a shipwreck, is often mentioned by the men who live on the island, but he has not been seen in recent years.

Another ghost presents himself every twenty-ninth of May, the anniversary of the execution of Charles I. This is the ghost of a regicide who died on Sable Island. Marching about the island with broad-brimmed hat and drawn sword, he sings psalm tunes in a nasal voice, which residents claim is heard even above the storm. As if these ghosts were not enough, lights are seen moving about old wrecks, and the muffled sounds of bells, as if tolling on sunken ships, are heard from the depths. For real shivers, one needs only recall the *Juno,* which many years ago drifted ashore, a corpse in the hold the vessel's only tenant.

Even the story of animal life on Sable Island is strange. The ponies which roam the island are guarded by patriarchal stallions, resembling the horses on the sculptures of Nineveh. Stocky, they are remarkable for their long manes, which have been known to grow to the length of three yards. At one time there were 500 wild ponies on the island, but their number has been decreased by exporting them. The importation of improved, domesticated stallions has made the stock less hardy and consequently more susceptible to death from exposure. At the last known count there were 310 wild ponies on Sable.

Mounted on partly-tamed ponies, the lifesavers gallop day and night over the dunes and among the hillocks on their long patrols. When a shipwreck occurs, the lifeboats are drawn to the scene by teams of five ponies, three at the shaft and two leaders. From time to time the wild ponies are sent to Halifax, where they are sold at auction for about fourteen to fifty dollars each.

Centuries ago the "Portingalls," or Portuguese, stocked the island with cattle. The cattle increased so rapidly that people from the mainland often made expeditions to the islands, returning with so much livestock that it made their trips extremely profitable. Then there was the time when the island was overrun with rabbits. Shortly afterward two rat-infested Norwegian vessels were wrecked. Swimming ashore, the rodents began to exterminate the rabbits and to attack the government stores. Cats were imported from Halifax to kill the rats, and after a while the cats increased so rapidly that dogs were imported to kill the cats. Between 1884 and 1896 the island was overrun with rats from more wrecked vessels, and when another cargo of cats was imported from Halifax, the cycle began again. This time, for some reason, after the cats ate the rats they did not multiply as before, and the situation has been more or less normal ever since. Once there were pigs on the island; but they have been exterminated because they became ghouls feasting on the remains of casta-

ways. Death in its most horrid form is often encountered at
Sable Island.

It is never very cold on the island—the temperature seldom
goes below six degrees above zero—but the dreadful storms
blow the sand about with great force. Through these gales of
sand the mounted patrolmen make their way, ever on the
alert for the booming of minute guns or other signals of distress from vessels which the treacherous shoals may be holding in their embrace of death.

Indeed, death is in evidence everywhere, with the island
itself engaged in an eternal fight with the sea for survival. It
seems as if it drew ships into its embrace to contain its loose
and shifting sand, thus protecting itself against annihilation.

Tradition says that when Sable Island was first discovered
by John Cabot in 1797, it was eighty miles long. In 1802,
when a rescue station was established there, officials estimated
that it was forty miles long. Although many Canadians believe the island will eventually wash away, Sable Island is
now longer than it was in 1884, with the latest survey indicating that it is twenty-four miles in length.

At one time, within a twenty-eight year period, the western
end lost seven miles. The West Light has been moved eastward five times since it was first established, the last move
being in 1947. Shoals over which the ocean now surges are
pointed out as former sites of lighthouses. One of them was
so swiftly undermined by the sea that it had to be abandoned
within a few hours during a storm. The location where once
stood the first superintendent's house is now under two fathoms of water!

On my last visit I climbed to the crest of a great hummock
of sand and stood there, looking far out toward the east. My

thoughts were of this island's experiences with the ocean. Slowly, like a ship dragging anchor, it moves eastward. I wondered if it would ever reach the edge of the shoals, stand tottering on the brink of the abyss, and then plunge forever into the depths? I recalled that some residents had told me that this gray sandy bay will slowly wear away until it becomes another submerged shoal, but I do not agree. My opinion is that there will always be a Sable Island in one form or another.

So many sunken vessels line the shoals of Sable Island that new wrecks pile up on the old. The *Crofton Hall*, an iron sailing ship wrecked shortly before the turn of the twentieth century on the northeast bar, broke in two amidships. The pieces drifted together again, and the islanders suppose that she struck crosswise on an old submerged wreck and settled over it, which accounts for the two parts coming together. Nor is the island satisfied with the awful tribute which it exacts from the living. The bark *John McLeod,* which was wrecked off Devil's Island at the entrance to Halifax Harbor, has drifted ashore on Sable Island bottom up, the wreck of a former wreck!

Everyone suggested that we extend our visit indefinitely, but we did not dare. If we had stayed a day or so extra, a quick change in the weather might have marooned us there an additional two or three months. And, as former superintendent D. S. Johnson told me once, in the winter the weather is a turncoat—big winds come from the northeast and northwest, and they are really vicious, snarling gales.

During the wintry storms and blizzards the island's wild horses get into a lee behind a dune and form a circle. The young and weak ponies stand in the middle and the stallions and older horses protect them on the outside.

There are many theories as to how the wild ponies and horses reached Sable Island, but the most probable explanation is that they are descendants of a cargo of animals sent to the island in 1760 by Thomas Hancock, uncle of the famous Revolutionary patriot John Hancock, for the benefit of ship-wrecked mariners.

After we had visited the entire island, we thought of our plans to fly back to the mainland, and then came the hour of departure. With just enough gas to travel 200 air miles, and Halifax 150 miles away, we had to be sure of reasonably good weather on the way back to the mainland. At two o'clock that day the prospects seemed favorable, and we all went down to the lake.

But we were not to get away from Sable Island's treacherous sands without a fight. As Ray Hylan gunned the engines, our plane rolled off the beach into ankle-deep water—and stuck fast in the soft sand. The islanders brought out horses and hitched them to the plane, but they could not pull us far enough for the aircraft to float free.

Finally we prevailed upon the islanders to lift the wings alternately to permit the retractable landing wheels to fold into the body of the plane. It took ten minutes to accomplish this, and every Sable Islander who helped got soaking wet. But it enabled the plane to get free of the sand and float on its hull. Roaring eastward toward the end of the lake, we took off safely and headed for Halifax. We made it by sun-set.

Just after the sun went down, pilot Ray Hylan, this time

with a lighted cigar in his mouth, smiled across at me as I sat in the copilot's seat.

"How about it, Ed, do you want to go back to Sable Island again?"

"Yes," came my answer, and it even surprised me. "You see, I've never been to Sable Island in the summertime and I'd like to try it."

There is an irresistible, terrible fascination to this isle of scores of unsolved mysteries.

CHAPTER 24

The *Thresher*

The nuclear submarine *Thresher* was lost with 129 persons aboard off the New England coast on April 10, 1963. Thus the nuclear age has provided its first tragic unsolved mystery of the sea. The submarine's destruction is indeed a vital mystery for the Navy and the shipbuilding profession to solve. The missing submarine probably hit bottom on what is called the Sohn Abyssal Plain of the Atlantic Ocean floor.

With the information about the submarine's last known position as 41.44 north and 64.57 west, it could be assumed that the *Thresher* settled down on the flat plain of the Atlantic seabed, at least 8,000 to 12,000 feet beneath the surface. The Sohm Plain site is just south and east of the Continental Rise and the Continental Shelf, the shallower ocean bed areas off our coast.

International Geophysical Year scientists studying the floors of the oceans, aided by modern sounding gear, have given the world an up-to-date idea of what we might see on the seabed. The ocean basin floor is divided into three groups: abyssal floor, oceanic rises, and seamounts. The latter are mountains in the sea. Two mountain peaks are Bermuda and the Azores.

On four other occasions New England waters have been the scene of American submarine disasters. The first occurred on September 25, 1925, off Block Island when the *S-51* was struck and sunk by the *City of Rome,* which was on her way to Boston. The second, the *S-4,* was off Provincetown, on December 16, 1927, and the third was off Portsmouth, New Hampshire, when the *Squalus* went down on May 23, 1939. The fourth, off the coast of Maine, took place June 20, 1941, when the submarine *O-9* went down with thirty-three men.

There were thirty-seven men aboard the *S-51* when she was hit by the steamer *City of Rome.* Although the lights of the *S-51* clearly indicated that she had the right of way, survivors said the steamer made no effort to obey the rules of the road and crashed into the submarine just forward of her conning tower. The *City of Rome* did not stop immediately, but a short time later she put over a boat and made a search of the area.

Meanwhile, aboard the *S-51* three men were able to cling to the deck until she went down and then were pulled aboard the lifeboat which had been launched by the steamer. Sixteen others drowned in the area, and eighteen men perished inside the submarine.

Several hours later, while approaching the entrance to the Cape Cod Canal, the *City of Rome* reported that she had run down and sunk the *S-51* off Block Island. When the submarine was finally brought to the surface weeks later, she was towed to the Brooklyn Navy Yard, where a large hole was revealed in her port side. The eighteen dead crewmen were found in the hull.

Two years later, on December 16, 1927, the submarine *S-4* was about to surface off the coast of Cape Cod. Three-quarters of a mile from the Wood End Lighthouse, Provincetown, the coast guard destroyer *Paulding* was approaching the same location. Just as the *S-4* broke the surface, the *Paulding* struck her, and the submarine sank at once.

Boatswain E. C. Gracie of Wood End Light witnessed the collision and launched a boat to go to the spot where he had last seen the submarine. On arriving over the *S-4*, he let down a line with a grapple attached but was unable to locate the submarine 100 feet below on the bottom.

Hour after hour passed, and finally, six and one-half hours after he began looking, Gracie located the smaller craft. Divers, who went down as soon as they could, were able to communicate with several men trapped inside the stricken vessel. One by one, however, the crew suffocated and died. The submarine was later towed to the Boston Navy Yard in Charlestown, where the forty dead were removed.

The *Squalus,* like its modern counterpart, was the newest and most-advanced attack submarine in the fleet when it left the Portsmouth Naval Shipyard for sea trials on May 23, 1939. She sank 240 feet off the Isle of Shoals near Rye Beach, New Hampshire.

The sinking of the *Squalus* held the attention of the world for two days as the most dramatic rescue operations were carried out to save the crew and civilian personnel. As the *Squalus* went down in 240 feet, rescue was possible with the use of a ten-ton diving bell that was dropped four times and came up with thirty-three survivors. Twenty-six others were lost.

For 113 days complex salvage operations were conducted by the Navy, and on September 13, 1939, the *Squalus* was brought to the surface. Repaired and rechristened the *Sailfish*, she was used in the Pacific campaign during World War II, where she performed admirably.

Little is known concerning New England's fourth undersea tragedy, that of the *O-9*. On June 20, 1941, during a test dive, the *O-9* exceeded the 212-foot safety depth limit for reasons never known, and her hull was soon crushed in. She sank to the bottom with all thirty-three men in her crew lost.

Since she was commissioned on July 27, 1918, the *O-9* was a veteran undersea craft. At the time of her sinking she was being used as a training ship. The craft was engaged in routine maneuvers in waters between 400 and 600 feet deep, and had previously been in a minor collision. When she was three hours overdue, public announcement was made of the fact of the sinking to the bottom of the Atlantic about fifteen miles off Portsmouth. It was about eighteen miles north of the place where the *Squalus* later went down.

Floating wreckage which came to the surface included bits of cork insulation, indicating (as in the case of the *Thresher* later) that at least one part of the venerable hull had been crushed. It was said at the time that if the men had attempted to use the Momsen lung when they made their way out of the submarine, their bodies would have collapsed and they would not have reached the surface alive.

The *O-9* had submerged at 8:36 that June morning and was to remain below surface until 10:36. At 10:40 her sister submarine, the *O-10*, sighted a black smoke bomb rising from the surface of the water in the southeast. Later a hard hat diver, Commander Robert Metzger, went down to a record 440 feet in an attempt to reach the *O-9*, but he did not see her. The *O-9* was never recovered, nor were the bodies of the thirty-three victims. A memorial service for those lost was held at the New London submarine base on June 24, 1941.

On the night of April 10, 1963, the U.S. Navy announced that the atomic submarine *Thresher* was "overdue and presumed missing" in the Atlantic. The *Thresher,* then conducting deep diving tests about 220 miles east of Boston, was the first attack submarine of her class and was rated as the world's fastest and deepest diving submersible. This was the Navy's first major accident involving an atomic submarine.

The Navy announcement said:

While there is a possibility that the nuclear submarine has not reported her position because of a communication failure, a search was immediately commenced by the Navy in accordance with emergency proceedings for such situations.

Navy ships, aircraft, and other submarines are searching the area where the *Thresher* was last reported. They are encountering cloudy weather and winds of from 25 to 40 knots and seas of from 5 to 9 feet. Such conditions would make it difficult for the on-scene search units to sight the overdue submarine even though it were on the surface and unable to transmit a position report by radio communications.

The location of the *Thresher* from her last report was given as 41.44 north and 64.57 west. The depth of water at this location is approximately 8,400 feet. Merchants ships in this area have been requested to look out for the submarine in addition to the maximum effort being made by the Navy.

Additional reports on the progress of the search will be made by the Navy. Names and addresses of members of the crew will be released after all next-of-kin have been notified that the ship is overdue.

The Navy said those aboard the *Thresher* included 16 officers, 96 enlisted men, and 17 civilians. Submarines, after leaving overhaul, often carry employees of the builder's yard for the purposes of the post-overhaul test, which accounts for the presence of the civilians. As an attack submarine the vessel would not be carrying Polaris missiles, the nuclear-capable weapon that can be launched from underwater by other submarines.

The *Thresher* was launched at Portsmouth, New Hampshire, Naval Shipyard, and was commissioned August 3, 1961. The Portsmouth yard in a pamphlet history published a year ago, described her as "the finest attack and killer submarine in the world." An improved version of the earlier nuclear submarine *Skipjack,* the *Thresher* combined "advanced sonar, deep depth, newer weapons, and emphasis on the elimination of noise as operating features." The 3,750-ton *Thresher* was 279 feet long.

The night the submarine was presumed lost four destroyers sped out of the cruiser-destroyer base at Newport at 7:00 P.M. on what was described as a "search and rescue" mission. Naval sources declined to give any further information on the mission, referring all inquiries to Washington. Unofficially, it was reported that the destroyers were headed into the Atlantic in search of the submarine that the Navy had reported overdue and presumed missing.

The nuclear attack submarine *Thresher* was constructed in

an approved "tear drop" design, distinguished by diving planes attached to the conning tower instead of the bow, as in most of her predecessors. She had torpedo tubes on both sides amidships, instead of at the bow.

The *Thresher* was said to be able to dive deeper and run more quietly at high speed than any other submarine. Her speed was classified, but it was believed to be about thirty-five knots. Her single screw, powered by a Westinghouse water-cooled nuclear reactor and a General Electric turbine, were said to be capable of driving her for 60,000 miles without refueling.

At the Portsmouth Navy Yard a board of inquiry was soon brought together under the jurisdiction of Vice Admiral Bernard L. Austin.

It was then announced that the *Thresher*, a $45,000,000 prototype of a projected submarine attack class of advanced design, was lost with 129 men aboard in 8,400 feet of water, 220 miles east of the Massachusetts coast, while undergoing sea trials following an extensive overhaul in the naval shipyard at Portsmouth.

Lieutenant (j.g.) James D. Watson, navigator of the *Skylark* which was escorting the *Thresher,* testified that he heard sounds like those "of a ship breaking up." He said he based his opinion on extensive submarine service in World War II, when he became familiar with the sounds of ships being torpedoed and sunk.

Lieutenant Commander Stanley W. Hecker, thirty-six, of Brooklyn, New York, the *Skylark*'s commander, gave the naval court of inquiry at Portsmouth his version of events, which mainly concerned a break in communications with the *Thresher* at 9:17 A.M. that Wednesday morning. He said that an underwater telephone was the only equipment he was able to use in meeting the situation that developed when the submarine *Thresher* was lost. On the other hand, Lieutenant Commander Hecker said he heard no sounds of the type Lieutenant Watson mentioned, but he acknowledged being unfamiliar with noises of that nature. The *Skylark*'s skipper otherwise corroborated the testimony given by Lieutenant Watson and two enlisted men.

Asked if he had discussed the projected sea trials with anyone from the missing submarine, Hecker said, "I had no agenda, except by telephone, beyond the official written orders to rendezvous with the *Thresher*. I had no information as to the capabilities of the *Thresher*, such as her depth, speed, and range. In fact, the U.Q.C. [underwater telephone] was the only equipment on the *Skylark* of known capability with submarines."

The captain of the *Skylark* then spoke of his feeling of helplessness at the time of the disaster. He addressed Vice Admiral Austin directly, "Admiral, I was willing to put down my four anchors, or even six anchors, every piece of line aboard, all my buoys or anything else to mark the spot, but I had only 7,200 feet of nylon line."

Commander Hecker, in his testimony, produced a series of working logs from the *Skylark*, covering the telephone, LORAN, or long range navigational aid, radio, and the navigator's work book.

The court particularly questioned the lieutenant commander about the events between 9:12 and 9:17 A.M. when the *Thresher* was last heard from. The *Skylark*'s skipper said he heard the message: "Experiencing minor problem, have position angle, attempting to blow." He described the voice from the *Thresher* as "very relaxed."

Hecker said that shortly afterward he distinctly heard sounds, with which he was familiar, of air being blown into a submarine's tanks to displace water and give the vessel more buoyancy. The *Skylark*'s commander said he later heard what appeared to be a voice trying to break through the noise of blowing air. He said he could not understand the words.

Other members of the *Skylark*'s crew said they heard "test depth" as part of a garbled message at 9:17, the last moment of communication. They also said that one other word might have been "exceeding."

Hecker also was questioned closely about an unidentified vessel sighted during a search of the area near where the *Thresher* went down. He described the craft as "of a dirty color, possibly gray once." The *Skylark* moved to within 6,000 yards of the vessel, which "seemed to be laying to." But he said he could not remember where she went after he had determined that she was not concerned with the search. The vessel was first thought to be a sail on a submarine, Hecker said, and "being anxious, we possibly hoped it was," he added.

During a brief afternoon session, Vice Admiral Elton W. Grenfell, commanding officer of the Atlantic Fleet submarines, told the court he had a theory concerning what happened to the *Thresher* but that it was in the area of military secrecy. He was permitted to present his views at a closed session.

Captain William Heronemus, shipbuilding and repair superintendent of the yard, told of 875 job orders issued during the nine months the *Thresher* was in the yard.

"I have known no other ship in a higher state of readiness for sea than the *Thresher*," he said.

A large piece of polyethylene plastic, found with the debris at the scene of the submarine's sinking, showed charred spots, indicating it was burned "in a rush of flame." The plastic piece, about eighteen inches square, was introduced as evidence at the hearings at the Portsmouth Naval Shipyard.

Frederick L. Downs, a chemist conducting tests on the debris, testified that the plastic was of the type commonly found in submarines of the *Thresher* class. He said it is used in the reactor shielding on nuclear-powered ships.

Downs stated that the plastic showed indications "that it had been in contact with a rush of flame." There were bits of metal embedded in it, he said. Also offered to the court were two orange pads about eighteen inches long, which appeared to be the stuffing from the inside of a lifejacket. The new debris was brought in a sea bag, and its nature was not disclosed until it was presented.

Also offered in evidence were eight other pieces of plastic, none larger than a man's hand. Downs said the edges appeared to be torn raggedly. The debris was found near the *Thresher*'s last known position and was introduced into evidence by Captain Samuel R. Heller, design superintendent at the Portsmouth yard and custodian for any debris found at the search scene.

The naval court went into closed session April 24, to hear and review evidence of a classified nature. The hearing room was cleared of newsmen shortly after an official of the Portsmouth Naval Shipyard where the submarine was built and overhauled was called to identify debris believed from the

Thresher. It was indicated that the testimony by Cicero A. Lewis, project engineer in the shipyard's design division, might deal with military secrets. Shortly before going into closed session, a veteran employee of the shipyard expressed the opinion that a failure in the *Thresher's* piping system might have triggered the sinking. James C. Rogers, an assistant quality assurance division superintendent at Portsmouth Naval Shipyard where the *Thresher* was built and overhauled, testified, "In my opinion failure of a piping system would be the most hazardous condition that might occur."

On April 23 the Navy lowered underwater cameras to the bottom of the Atlantic to see if they could find the hulk of the missing submarine. They located about a dozen objects on the ocean floor, 8,400 feet deep, in the area where the *Thresher* disappeared. The Navy said six of these objects "look like real good prospects." The search was narrowed to an area of 10 square miles 270 miles east of Boston. The Navy said it was confident that the sunken attack submarine lay somewhere within that area.

In another development the chairman of the Joint Congressional Committee, Senator John O. Pastore, said the *Thresher* investigation indicated that the cause of the disaster would ultimately be "reasonably well" established. He made his statement after two members of the joint committee briefed committeemen on the work of a naval court of inquiry investigating the *Thresher.*

Captain C. B. Bishop, a submarine expert in the Office of the Chief of Naval Operations, said it was possible that cameras lowered from the survey ship *Atlantis* would soon find the *Thresher.*

Supervisors and mechanics at Portsmouth Naval Shipyard

had been disciplined at least twice for improper or sloppy work during the nine-month overhaul of the lost submarine, it was disclosed to the naval court of inquiry. The court was also told by a former crewman that a spike and "an awful lot of dirt and crud" were found in the air filter system of the sub's engine room during an overhaul several months ago.

Torpedoman 1st class Raymond Mattson, thirty-three, of Chisholm, Minnesota, who was transferred from the *Thresher* the day before she left on her last cruise, testified that the submarine came back to Portsmouth for an overhaul after a number of defects, including a leak, came to light during diving tests off Florida.

On April 15 the men and machines of the Portsmouth Naval Shipyard paused for half an hour to pay their final respects to the 129 persons who were lost on the *Thresher*. A crowd estimated at more than five thousand gathered around the mall of the yard to hear prayers and eulogies from chaplains of three faiths and officials of the federal government. Widows and children of the naval personnel and civilian technicians aboard the *Thresher* occupied seats of honor before the conning tower of the submarine *Squalus*, which also served as a pulpit. In a front row seat was Mrs. John W. Harvey, widow of Lieutenant Commander Harvey, commanding officer of the *Thresher*.

Kenneth E. Belieu, an assistant secretary of the Navy, read a message from Secretary of Defense Robert S. McNamara. The bereaved relatives, the secretary's message said, had "some means of comfort from knowing their men died serving their country."

Rear Admiral J. Floyd Dreith, director of the chaplain's

division of the Navy, said there could be "no higher honor or glory than was accorded these men on the altar of human dignity and freedom throughout the world."

After the ceremony, a three-foot wreath of white chrysanthemums in the shape of the *Thresher* was taken to Pease Air Force Base in nearby Newington, New Hampshire, then flown to sea and dropped where a buoy marked the approximate spot where the ship went down.

More than five months have elapsed since the *Thresher* disappeared on April 10, 1963 as I write my final words for this chapter. The Navy's deep sea diving craft *Trieste* has made dive after dive in search of the lost submarine.

When I went aboard the *Trieste* with Commander George Bailey of the U.S.S. *Preserver* he explained to me how the *Trieste* operates. The most amazing facts to me were that aviation gas and B-B shot are loaded aboard for ballast.

I was informed that the position of the *Thresher* is 270 miles due east of Boston. There are many theories, of course, as to what happened to her, but it is generally conceded that some fitting let go, allowing salt water to enter the hull under great pressure.

Gradually the power failed, battery and nuclear, and as the craft went down and down the pressure crushed in the sides of the submarine. It is believed by some that the speed of the *Thresher* on her way to the bottom became faster and faster until she may have hit the bottom at a rate of 125 knots!

Identifiable debris is all over the area. One large fragment, said to be about twenty by ten feet, has been seen. A boot has been photographed which was seen to have the *Thresher*'s nuclear mark, number five, on it. A pipe, which had the *Thresher*'s number 593, engraved on it, was brought up from the bottom. It is about three feet long, and was "utterly and totally collapsed." This pipe came from inside the pressure hull and was not an external part.

Many details of this disaster, however, may always be shrouded in mystery.

A list of the 129 lost on the *Thresher* follows:

OFFICERS:

Lt. (j.g.) Ronald Babcock
Lt. Comdr. Michael J. DiNola
Lt. Comdr. Pat M. Garner
Lt. (j.g.) John G. Grafton
Lt. Comdr. John W. Harvey
   (Captain of *Thresher*)
Lt. (j.g.) James J. Henry, Jr.
Lt. Comdr. John S. Lyman, Jr.
Lt. (j.g.) Frank J. Malinski

Lt. (j.g.) Guy C. Parsons, Jr.
Lt. John Smarz, Jr.
Lt. (j.g.) John J. Wiley
Lt. Merrill F. Collier
Lt. Comdr. Philip H. Allen
Lt. Comdr. John H. Billings
Lt. Robert D. Biederman
Lt. Comdr. Robert L. Krag

ENLISTED MEN:

Tilmon J. Arsenault
Ronald E. Bain
John E. Bell
Edgar S. Bobbitt
Gerald C. Boster
George Bracey
Richard P. Brann
Richard J. Carkoski
Patrick Wayne Carmody
Steven G. Cayey
Edward Christiansen
Larry W. Claussen

Thomas E. Clements
Francis M. Cummings
Samuel J. Dabruzzi
Clyde E. Davidson
Donald C. Day
Roy O. Denny
Peter Dibella
Don R. Dundas
Troy E. Dyer
Elwood H. Forni
Raymond B. Foti
Gregory J. Fusco

Andrew J. Gallant, Jr.
Napoleo T. Garcia
John E. Garner
Robert W. Gaynor
Robert H. Gosnell
William E. Graham
Aaron J. Gunter
Richard C. Hall
Norman T. Hayes
Laird Glenn Heiser
Marvin Theodore Helsius
Leonard Hogentogler Hewitt
James P. Hodge
Joseph Harshorne Hodge
John F. Hudson
John P. Inglis
Brawner G. Johnson
Richard L. Johnson
Robert E. Johnson
Thomas B. Johnson
Richard W. Jones
Edmund J. Kaluza, Jr.
Thomas C. Kantz
Robert D. Kearney
Ronald D. Keiler
George J. Kiesecker
Billy M. Kiler
George Ronald Kroner
Norman G. Lanouette
Wayne W. Lavoie
Templeman N. Mabry
Richard N. Mann, Jr.
Douglas R. McCelland
Donald J. McCord
Karl P. McDonough

Sidney L. Middleton
Julius F. Marullo, Jr.
Ronald A. Muise
James A. Musselwhite
Donald E. Nault
Walter Jack Noonis
John D. Norris
Chesley C. Oetting
Roscoe C. Pennington
James G. Peters
James F. Phillippi
Dan A. Philput
Richard Podwell
John S. Regan
James P. Ritchie
Pervis Robison
Glenn A. Rountree
Anthony W. Rushetski
James M. Schiewe
Benjamin N. Shafer
John D. Shafer
Joseph T. Shimko
Burnett M. Shotwell
Alan D. Sinnett
William H. Smith, Jr.
James L. Snider
Ronald H. Solomon
Robert E. Steinel
Roger E. Van Pelt
David A. Wasel
Joseph A. Walski
Charles L. Wiggins
Donald E. Wise
Ronald E. Wolfe
Jay H. Zweifel

CIVILIANS:

Fred P. Abrams
Daniel W. Beal, Jr.
Robert E. Charron
K. R. Corcoran
Kenneth J. Critchley
Paul C. Currier
George J. Dineen
Richard R. Des Jardins
Richard K. Fisher

Paul A. Guerette
Maurice F. Jaquay
D. Kuester
Henry Moreau
Franklin J. Palmer
Robert D. Prescott
D. Stadtmuller
Laurence E. Whitten

OTHER MEMBERS OF CREW NOT ABOARD AT TIME:

Lt. Raymond A. McCoole—on annual leave, sick wife
Torpedo Mate 1st class Raymond C. Mattson—on annual leave
Chief Machinist Mate Frank J. Destefan, Jr.—temporary duty in
  Washington

Index